IMAGES OF WAR

The F-4 Phantom

IMAGES OF WAR

The F-4 Phantom

RARE PHOTOGRAPHS FROM WARTIME ARCHIVES

MARTIN W. BOWMAN

Pen & Sword
AVIATION

First published in Great Britain in 2019 by
Pen & Sword Aviation
an imprint of
Pen & Sword Books Ltd
Yorkshire – Philadelphia

ISBN 978 1 52670 576 1

A CIP catalogue record for this book is available from the British Library.

Typeset in 12/14.5 Gill Sans by
Aura Technology and Software Services, India.

Printed and bound by CPI UK.

Pen & Sword Books Limited incorporates the imprints of Atlas, Archaeology, Aviation, Discovery, Family History, Fiction, History, Maritime, Military, Military Classics, Politics, Select, Transport, True Crime, Air World, Frontline Publishing, Leo Cooper, Remember When, Seaforth Publishing, The Praetorian Press, Wharncliffe Local History, Wharncliffe Transport, Wharncliffe True Crime and White Owl.

For a complete list of Pen & Sword titles please contact

PEN & SWORD BOOKS LIMITED
47 Church Street, Barnsley, South Yorkshire, S70 2AS, England
E-mail: enquiries@pen-and-sword.co.uk
Website: www.pen-and-sword.co.uk

Or
PEN AND SWORD BOOKS
1950 Lawrence Rd, Havertown, PA 19083, USA
E-mail: Uspen-and-sword@casematepublishers.com
Website: www.penandswordbooks.com

Contents

Acknowledgements

Once again Joe Baugher's serial number listings proved indispensible, as did various other websites including the fabulous 'USS Coral Sea Tribute Website'. Publications too numerous to mention include this author's *Combat Legends: F-4 Phantom* (The Crowood Press/Airlife 2003) and *The Men Who Flew the F-4 Phantom* (Pen & Sword Aviation (2017) while in my opinion *The Phantom Story* by Anthony M. Thornborough and Peter E. Davies (Arms & Armour Press, 1994) is the most comprehensive volume of all.

Introduction

Capable of Mach 2.2, the McDonnell F-4 Phantom II resulted from a requirement for a two-seat, twin-engine, shipboard fighter, originally ordered in 1954 as a single-seat AH-1 attack aircraft. Probably the most famous of all the aircraft to emerge from the post-Korea era, the world's first truly multi-role supersonic combat aircraft was born when the US Navy placed a letter of intent for a new shipboard fighter on 18 October 1954. Few could have foreseen the multitude of roles this most successful of post-war fighters would fulfil. As early as 1955, changes in specification altered the Phantom's primary role from a twin-engined strike aircraft to that of a long-range, high-altitude interceptor. The XF4H-1 made its maiden flight on 27 May 1958 and delivery to the US Navy began in February 1960 for carrier trials. Fleet deliveries of the 'Great Smoking Thunderhog' began on 8 July 1961 when VF-74's 'Bedevilers' at NAS Oceana, Virginia began receiving F-4Bs. The USN operated the F4H-1 (re-designated F-4A in 1962), a total of forty-five of which were built. None saw combat and most ended up as test or training aircraft. All in all, the Phantom set sixteen world time-to-height, speed and endurance records. Except for Project 'Skyburner', all records were achieved in unmodified production aircraft. Five of the speed records remained unbeaten until the F-15 Eagle appeared in 1975. In all, 1,218 Phantom IIs have been supplied to the US Navy with a further forty-six to the USMC.

The first Phantom to equip the USAF was the F-4C tactical fighter developed from the US Navy F-4B, which was found to outperform all USAF fighters by a wide margin. Almost identical to the naval Phantom (a result of Defense Secretary Robert McNamara's policy of encouraging equipment commonality among the Services) but unlike the naval version, the F-4C had dual controls, an inertial navigation system, J79-GE-15 turbojets and provision for a large external weapons load; it was fitted with a boom-type flight refuelling system with receptacle on top of the fuselage instead of the Navy's probe and drogue system with its retractable prove on the starboard side of the forward fuselage. Altogether, 583 F-4Cs were built, equipping sixteen of the twenty-three Tactical Air Command wings in a variety of roles including close-support, attack and air superiority.

Just twelve early production F-4Bs were converted to F-4G standard. They were fitted with an approach power compensation system for use in a new automatic carrier landing mode, and the RCA AN/ASW-21 two-way digital data-link communications equipment in an attempt to automate the air defence process between ships, AEW aircraft and fighters. (Both these features were standard on the F-4J.) BuNo150481, the first F-4G, flew on 20 March 1963. The twelve converted aircraft were delivered to VF-96 'Fighting Falcons' at NAS Miramar in mid-1963 for trials. Finally, in October 1965, these went to sea with VF-213 'Black Lions' aboard the USS *Kitty Hawk* for deployment in the Gulf of Tonkin. After returning to the USA, the remaining F-4Gs were remanufactured to F-4B standard and the F-4G designation was re-used in 1978 for the 'Wild Weasel' variant of the F-4E. The back seater or GIB (Guy In Back) on a 'Wild Weasel' was called 'the bear' and the back seat was called the 'bear pit'.

The F-4D, which was developed from the F-4C and introduced improved weapons delivery systems, flew for the first time on 7 December 1965 and service deliveries to the USAF began in March 1966, examples first reaching combat units in Viêtnam in 1967. Eventually all F-4Cs in theatre were replaced by the F-4D. In all, 843 F-4Ds were built and some equipped the air forces of Iran and the Republic of Korea.

The F-4E, which first flew on 30 June 1967, was a multi-role fighter designed for the close-support, interdiction and air-superiority roles with a 20 mm Vulcan rotary cannon (a Gatling gun capable of firing 1,200 rounds in the space of twelve seconds and known as 'the pistol') in an enormous cigar-shaped pod under the belly of the aircraft. In the intercept role, the 'E' could carry four or six AIM-7E plus four AIM-9D air-to-air missiles. Internally, it carried an additional fuselage fuel tank, improved fire-control and target guidance systems, and leading-edge slats were retro-fitted to improve manoeuvrability.

The F-4J had improved air-to-air and ground-attack capability; deliveries began in 1966 and ended in 1972 with 522 built. The F-4N (updated F-4Bs) with smokeless engines and F-4J aerodynamic improvements began in 1972 under a US. Navy-initiated refurbishment programme called 'Project Bee Line' with 228 converted by 1978. The F-4S model resulted from the refurbishment of 265 F-4Js with J79-GE-17 smokeless engines of 17,900 lb and other improvements. The USMC also operated the RF-4B with reconnaissance cameras with forty-six built.

In the mid-1970s the USAF and General Dynamics jointly embarked on programmes aimed at producing a Phantom reconnaissance aircraft capable of operating as high as 76,000 feet or above the ceiling of the MiG-25 'Foxbat'. These programmes were apparently undertaken either following the decision not to export the Martin RB-57F high-altitude reconnaissance aircraft to Israel or/and when it became evident, in 1972, that the carriage of the HIAC-1 camera pod by the F-4 would result in unacceptable performance penalties. F-4E 69-7576 was modified to carry the General Dynamics HIAC-1 LOROP camera of 66-inch focal length operating through side and bottom-mounted oblique windows, altering the nose shape and increasing fuselage length by 12 inches; however, without a USAF requirement for the RF-4X or its proposed F-4X fighter variant, development costs were soon found to be too high to justify manufacture of a few aircraft for the IDF/AF. The project never reached prototype stage and 69-7576 was modified to F-4E(S) configuration.

The Phantom was also the only aircraft used by both US flight demonstration teams: the USAF 'Thunderbirds', which used the F-4E from the 1969 season until 1974, and the US Navy 'Blue Angels', which transitioned to the F-4J in 1969. In December 1974 the Navy Flight Demonstration Team downsized to the subsonic Douglas A-4F Skyhawk and was reorganised into the Navy Flight Demonstration Squadron.

F-4N BuNo150438 of VF-154 'Black Knights' over the USS *Coral Sea* in 1983. (USS Coral Sea Tribute Website)

F-4N BuNo160423 of VF-154 'Black Knights' launches off the angle deck aboard USS *Coral Sea* CV-43 in December 1981. (USS Coral Sea Tribute Website)

CHAPTER 1

US Navy and USMC

In South East Asia, North Viêtnamese MiGs, equipped with both cannons and missiles, often outmanoeuvred the heavier F-4, which though faster was not as agile; American pilots were also not trained for close range dogfights, as the Air Force assumed air-to-air engagements would occur at long range with missiles. Furthermore, the J79 engines produced thick black smoke, which combined with the F-4's larger size, made it easier to spot and target from a distance. Rules of engagement in Viêtnam prohibited US pilots from shooting at unidentified targets beyond visual range, further crippling the advantages of the missiles. New J79 engines cured the problem of the F-4's visible black smoke and eventually, the Air Force upgraded all of its F-4Es with wing-slats that significantly improved manoeuvrability at a slight cost in speed. In 1968, following research into the failings of the US air-to-air missiles used in combat in Operation 'Rolling Thunder' (2 March 1965 to 1 November 1968), which ultimately resulted in almost 1,000 US aircraft lost in about one million sorties, the USAF concluded that its air losses were primarily due to unobserved MiG attacks from the rear and were, therefore, a technological problem. The Air Force responded by upgrading its F-4 fleet, installing an internal M61 Vulcan cannon (replacing the gun pods that vibrated excessively when carried under the aircraft's belly), developing improved airborne radar systems and working to solve the targeting problems of the AIM-9 and AIM-7 air-to-air missiles. The Navy concluded that air-crew training in air combat manoeuvering (ACM) was inadequate and recommended the establishment of an 'Advanced Fighter Weapons School' to revive fighter expertise. The school, popularly known as 'Top Gun', was established on 3 March 1969 at Naval Air Station Miramar, California using many F-4 and F-8 pilots as instructors and placed under the control of the VF-121 'Pacemakers' an F-4-equipped Replacement Air Group (RAG) unit. Navy pilots went on to score a superior kill ratio in Viêtnam of forty victories for seven aircraft lost to enemy aircraft in air-to-air combat. According to the USN, their kill-to-loss ratio against the North Viêtnamese Air Force (NVAF) MiGs soared from 3.7:1 (1965-1967) to 13:1 (after 1970) while the Air Force, which had not implemented a similar training programme, actually had its kill ratio worsen for a time after the resumption of bombing. US Navy Phantom squadrons took part in eighty-four combat tours with F-4Bs, F-4Js and F-4Ns, losing seventy-three Phantoms in combat (including thirteen to SAMs and fifty-three to AAA). An additional fifty-four Phantoms were lost in non-combat mishaps. USAF Phantoms claimed 107 air-to-air kills for thirty-three lost to MiGs and the Marine Corps claimed three. Ground fire shot down 474 Phantoms in all services.

Phantoms first reached the Naval Air Reserve in 1969 when F-4Bs were assigned to VF-22L1 at NAS Los Alamitos, California. In 1970, four reserve fighter squadrons - VF-201 and VF-202 (USN) with the Atlantic Fleet and VF-301 and VF-302 with the Pacific Fleet - were established, but they were at first equipped with the Ling- Temco-Vought F-8 Crusader because active units urgently needed F-4s. In 1974, F-4Bs finally replaced the Crusaders and they were in turn replaced by F-4N and F-4S Phantoms. The last F-4N was flown by VF-201 'Rangers' from NAS Dallas, Texas to Naval Air Technical Training Center (NATTC) Memphis, Tennessee on 29 February 1984. The last F-4S (155560) was retired by VF-202 'Superheats' at NAS Dallas on 14 May 1987. The Naval Air Test Center (NATC) and the Naval Test Pilot School (NTPS) operated F-4s at NAS Patuxent River in the period 1958-88. They also served in a wide range of experimental roles, mainly at NAS Point Mugu (with VX-4); NAS China Lake and NAF El Centro, California; NASWC/NWEC Kirtland AFB, New Mexico; and Naval Air Development Center (NADC) Johnsville, Pennsylvania.

In 1984 the USN F-4Ns had been retired and by 1987, the last F-4Ss were retired in the US Navy deployable squadrons. On 25 March 1986, an F-4S of VF-151 'Vigilantes' became the last active duty USN Phantom to launch from an aircraft carrier from *Midway*. On 18 October 1986, an F-4S of VF-202 'Superheats', a Naval Reserve fighter squadron, made the last-ever Phantom carrier landing while operating aboard *America*. In 1987 the last of the Naval Reserve-operated F-4S aircraft were replaced by F-14As. The last Phantoms in service with the Navy were QF-4 target drones operated by the Pacific Missile Test Center (PMTC) Point Mugu and Naval Weapons Center (NWC) China Lake. These airframes were subsequently retired in 2004.

The Marine Corps received its first F-4Bs in June 1962, the 'Black Knights' of VMFA-314 at Marine Corps Air Station El Toro, California becoming the first operational squadron. Phantoms of VMFA-531 'Gray Ghosts' were assigned to Đà Nẵng Air Base on South Viêtnam's north-east coast on 10 May 1965 and were initially assigned to provide air defence for the USMC. They soon began close air support missions (CAS) and VMFA-314 'Black Knights', VMFA-232 'Red Devils, VMFA-323 'Death Rattlers' and VMFA-542 'Bengals' soon arrived at the primitive airfield. Marine F-4 pilots claimed three enemy MiGs (two while on exchange duty with the USAF) at the cost of seventy-five aircraft lost in combat, mostly to ground fire and four in accidents. VMCJ-1 'Golden Hawks' flew the first RF-4B photo-recon mission on 3 November 1966 from Đà Nẵng and remained there until 1970. The F-4 continued to equip fighter-attack squadrons in both Marine Corps active and reserve units until the early 1990s. In the early 1980s, these squadrons began to transition to the F/A-18 Hornet. On 18 January 1992, the last Marine Corps Phantom, an F-4S in the Marine Corps Reserve was retired by the 'Cowboys' of VMFA-112, after which the squadron was re-equipped with F/A-18 Hornets.

The revised mock-up of the F-4H in December 1955 with provision for J79 engines and four radar-guided AIM-7 Sparrow missiles. The original mock-up of the AH-1 had a single seat cockpit and flat wing and tailplane configuration. (McDonnell-Douglas)

F4H-1F Phantoms (redesignated F-4A in 1962 on the line at St. Louis in October 1960). Nearest the camera is BuNo148266, which while with VF-101 'Grim Reapers' crashed while landing at NAS Key West, Florida on 30 April 1964. (McDonnell-Douglas)

The 5,000th Phantom II (F-4E 77-0290 for the Turkish Air Force) with James Smith McDonnell at St Louis on 9 May 1978. After twenty-four years of continuous production Phantom II production ended in the United States in 1979 after 5,195 had been built (5,057 by McDonnell Douglas and 138 in Japan by Mitsubishi). Of these, 2,874 went to the USAF, 1,264 to the Navy and Marine Corps and the rest to foreign customers. The last US-built F-4 went to South Korea, while the last F-4 built was an F-4EJ built by Mitsubishi Heavy Industries in Japan and delivered on 20 May 1981. (McDonnell-Douglas)

A3D-2 of VAH-8 'Smokin' Tigers' from the USS *Saratoga* refuelling F-4B-1F BuNo148261 of VAH-9 Saratoga Project LANA on 24 May 1961. For Project LANA (L for the Roman numeral 50 and ANA for the Anniversary of Naval Aviation), five F4H-IFs, competing for the Bendix Trophy, took off at timed intervals from Ontario, California and flew to NAS Brooklyn (Floyd Bennett Field), New York. In four supersonic dashes at altitudes of 50,000 feet, separated by three subsonic flight refuellings at 35,100 feet from tanker-configured A3D-2 Skywarriors, three of the Phantoms, flown by USN crews, reached New York having shattered the previous record (3 hours 8 minutes set in November 1957 by a USAF RF-101C). The best time - for which the team of Lieutenant Richard F. Gordon, pilot and Lieutenant (j.g.) Bobbie R. Young, RIO of VF-121 received the Bendix Trophy - was 2 hours 47 minutes. This represented an average speed of 870 mph over the 2,446-mile flight. While with VF 101, BuNo143392 was written off at NAS Key West, Florida on 16 October 1964 after the nose gear collapsed during landing and the aircraft caught fire. It has been displayed at NAS Oceana, Virginia wearing different serials and markings over many years.

F-4H-1 BuNo148419 of VF-121 'Pacemakers' off the Californian coast in 1962. This Phantom crashed on take-off from NAS Miramar, California on 13 May 1963 when the pilot attempted to rotate at too low speed. Lieutenant Commander J. F. Nichols ejected safely. His RIO (Radar Intercept Officer) remained with the aircraft and suffered no injuries. (USN)

F-4B BuNo148421 of VF-96 'Fighting Falcons' intercepting a Tu-16 in 1963. While with VF-101 'Grim Reapers' on 7 June 1971, this Phantom was lost at sea 200 miles ESE of NAS Oceana following structural failure and loss of control. Both crew were recovered. (USN)

F-4B 148415 of VMF(AW)-513 'Flying Nightmares' in the USS *Constellation* in 1963. This Phantom went to the MASDC (Military Aircraft Storage and Disposition Center) or 'bone yard' at Davis-Monthan AFB, Arizona (now AMARG - Aerospace Maintenance and Regeneration Group) as '8F0030' on 26 September 1973. It was SOC (Struck Off Charge) on 25 August 1977 and converted to QF-4B, being expended on 20 September 1983. (USMC)

F-4B BuNo149410 of VF-96 'Fighting Falcons' performs a touch-and-go landing aboard HMS *Hermes* on 17 January 1963. VF-96 was assigned to Carrier Air Group 9 aboard the USS *Ranger* to the Western Pacific from 9 November 1962 to 14 June 1963. Note the Fairey Gannet AEW.3 of B Flight, 849 Naval Air Squadron parked next to the island. The small size of this ship and of the other smaller carriers in the Royal Navy's fleet meant that only *Eagle* and *Ark Royal* were of sufficient size to operate the Phantom successfully. While serving with VMFA-115 'Silver Eagles', BuNo149410 crashed into Monkey Mountain, South Viêtnam in bad weather on 26 October 1965. Both crewmen were killed. (USN)

Above: F-4Bs of VF-114 'Aardvarks' escort a Soviet Tu-16 'Badger' as it passes over the carrier *Kitty Hawk* in January-February 1964 during Exercise 'Picture Window III'. (USN)

Opposite above: F-4N BuNo153023 of VMFA-531 'Gray Ghosts' landing on the deck of USS *Coral Sea* in the Arabian Sea in 1963. Following the Gulf of Tonkin incident in August, *Coral Sea* departed on 7 December 1964 for duty with the Seventh Fleet. Navy Phantoms first saw action in SE Asia when F-4Bs of CVW-14 on *Constellation* escorted the first Navy strike on 4 August 1964. The Phantom's arrival in theatre was very opportune because although at that time the NVASF had no fighters (they first appeared ion 3 April 1965), by the end of the year thirty-four MiG-17s were available and by June 1965, this number had increased to seventy. The *Coral Sea* continued to make WestPac/Viêtnam deployments until 1975. BuNo153023 was written off on the USS *Coral Sea* on 3 April 1983. (USMC)

Opposite below: F-4B BuNo152975 of VMFA-531 'Gray Ghosts' on USS *Coral Sea* in the Arabian Sea in 1963. This Phantom went to MASDC (as 8F0129) on 19 October 1983 and it was salvaged in November 2004. (USMC)

VMFA-531
3023
MARINES
206

VMFA-531
2975
MARINES
202
00

F-4B of VF-31 'Tomcatters' landing on USS *Saratoga* in 1964. VF-31 was assigned to Carrier Air Wing 3 (CVW-3) aboard the 'Super Sara' for a deployment to the Mediterranean from 28 November 1964 to 12 July 1965. Altogether, seventeen attack carriers (ten from the Pacific Fleet and seven from the Atlantic Fleet) were used in operations during the Viêtnam War. The first air combat victory in SE Asia was made on 9 April 1965 when two F-4Bs of VF-96 'Fighting Falcons' from the USS *Ranger* destroyed two MiG-17 'Fresco's of the Chinese Air Force. (USN)

F-4Bs of VF-84 'Jolly Rogers' on the USS *Independence* in 1964. BuNo149474 was WFU (Withdrawn From Use) at NAS Oceana, Virginia in 1972 and assigned as a ground trainer at NAS Miramar, California. 149465 was SOC on 26 August 1977 and in 1984 was put into storage at NAS North Island, California. 149466 was converted to QF-4B drone as '41' and was expended on 17 May 1974. (USN)

F-4B BuNo151485 of VF-21 'Freelancers' from the USS *Midway* uses standard dive-bombing technique against a North Viêtnamese target in 1965. The bombs are 500 lb Mk.82 Snakeyes with retarding fins that pop out after launch. The F-4B was the only Marine aircraft which could carry two 2,000 lb bombs and proved well suited for the ground attack role in Việtnam where on average loads of 5,000 lb were carried. *Midway* sailed for the Far East on 6 March 1965, and from mid-April, flew strikes against military and logistics installations in North and South Viêtnam. On 17 June 1965, aviators of *Midway*'s Attack Carrier Wing 2, VF-21 'Freelancers' downed the first two MiGs credited to US forces in SE Asia. From 1965-1970, the eleven USMC F-4B squadrons operated on a rotational basis from Đà Nẵng and Chu Lai in support of USMC ground forces in South Việtnam, and on 'Tally Ho' offensive strikes in the North Việtnamese panhandle and 'Steel Tiger'/'Tiger Hound' interdiction sorties in Laos. While with VF-92 'Silver Kings', BuNo151485 crashed into the Gulf of Tonkin due to battle damage on 7 May 1968. (USN)

F-4B BuNo150482 VF-21 'Freelancers' from the USS *Midway* off Viêtnam. On 18 May 1971 after relieving *Hancock* on Yankee Station, *Midway* began single carrier operations. *Midway* departed Yankee Station on 5 June, completing the vessel's final line period on 31 October 1971. With embarked Carrier Air Wing 5 (CVW 5), *Midway* again departed Alameda for operations off Viêtnam on 10 April 1972, continuing operations during 'Linebacker' throughout that summer. On 12 January 1973 a combat aircraft from *Midway* made the last air-to-air kill of the Viêtnam War. Later upgraded to F-4N, BuNo150482 served with VF-41 'Black Aces' onboard the *Independence* from 10 May to 13 December 1965 and also served on VF-111 'Sundowners', finally going to MASDC (as 8F0158) on 7 February 1984 before being converted to a QF-4N drone. It was expended in a missile test on 13 April 1996. (USN)

Above: F-4B BuNo152218 of VF-21 'Freelancers' from the USS *Midway*. On 10 January 1966 while with VMFA-323 'Death Rattlers', BuNo152218 crashed near Phước Bình, 20 miles south of Đà Nẵng after being caught in a premature blast of its own bombs. Both crew survived. (USN)

Opposite above: F-4Bs of VMFA-115 'Silver Eagles' and VMFA-323 'Death Rattlers' in MAG-11 at Đà Nẵng, probably in late 1965. At the end of the Viêtnam War, Phantoms remained the only fighter aircraft in service with the Fleet Marine Force until the arrival of the first F/A-18 Hornets in January 1983. The last F-4Ss were finally phased out early in 1989, the last being VMFA-134 at MCAS El Toro, California which received F/A-18As in spring 1989. In the Marine Air Reserve, F-4Bs were first delivered in December 1973 to VMFA-321 at NAF Washington. F-14As progressively replaced F-4Bs and F-4Js in most deployable squadrons, except the six squadrons assigned to the older and smaller CVAs' USS *Midway*, *Franklin D. Roosevelt* and *Coral Sea*, which were eventually re-equipped with F-4N/S Phantoms. (USMC)

Opposite below: F-4G 150645 of VF-213 'Black Lions' (pictured in 1965) was one of twelve F-4Bs converted to F-4G, on 26 April 1964. This was the first and only F-4G lost in SE Asia when on 28 April 1966, it was hit by ground fire as it was making a rocket attack on some cargo-carrying junks about two miles off the North Viêtnamese coast, 15 miles north-east of Thành Hòa and crashed into Gulf of Tonkin. The aircraft caught fire, the port engine was shut down and fuel was seen to be streaming from the aircraft. As the aircraft flew towards the *Kitty Hawk*, the fire spread and when the starboard engine also had to be shut down, the crew ejected and were picked up by a Navy helicopter 60 miles from the coast. (USN)

WS
0648
MARINES
VE
MARINES

NH
0645
VF-213
NAVY
111

Above: F-4B BuNo148430 of VF-114 'Aardvarks', part of Attack Carrier Air Wing Seven on the USS *Kitty Hawk* in 1965. Rear Admiral William F. Bringle assumed command of Carrier Division Seven on 6 April 1964, additionally serving as Commander Task Group 77.6 from 29 March to 29 June 1965 and as Commander Task Force 77 from 28 May to 27 June 1965. Between 1963 and 1975, the 'Aardvarks' made nine cruises to Viêtnam and the Western Pacific, all aboard the USS *Kitty Hawk*. BuNo148430 went to MASDC (as 8F0011) on 14 December 1971 and was assigned as a battle damage repair trainer at Hill AFB, Utah in September 1980. (USN)

Opposite above: F-4Bs of VF-213 'Black Lions' being bombed up aboard the *Kitty Hawk* off Viêtnam in 1966. For approximately two months in 1966, Carrier Air Wing camouflage trials embarked on *Kitty Hawk* and *Constellation* used aircraft painted in standard USAF overall dark green camouflage scheme experimentally to reduce losses from ground fire over Viêtnam. This was not successful on the *Kitty Hawk*'s aircraft and the results did not warrant a general change. (USN)

Opposite below: F-4B BuNo151506 of VF-154 'Black Knights' on the USS *Coral Sea* in 1967. While with VF-154 on the USS *Constellation* on 10 January 1968 151506 collided in midair with BuNo151499 in the South China Sea. All four crewmen were rescued. During 1968-69, 1969-70 and 1970-71 on WestPac cruises aboard USS *Ranger*, VF-154 was equipped with the F-4J. Beginning with their 16 November 1972 deployment, when they undertook the squadron's final Viêtnam cruise, onboard *Ranger*, VF-154 participated in some of the last US Navy strikes of the war and they received the Clifton Award - recognising them as the best fighter squadron in the United States Navy. (USN)

On 29 July 1967, one of the greatest tragedies of the war in SE Asia occurred as the result of a simple electrical malfunction. The Atlantic Fleet carrier *Forrestal* had left Norfolk, Virginia on 6 June after a major refit and was assigned to TF 77 on 8 July. After working up in the South China Sea, the *Forrestal* took up her position at 'Yankee Station' on 25 July for her combat debut off Việtnam. Four days later, after flying just 150 combat sorties, she was limping away from Việtnam towards Subic Bay in the Philippines for temporary repairs before returning to Norfolk, Virginia on 14 September for a major refurbishment. On the morning of 29 July as a launch was under way, a stray voltage ignited a Zuni rocket pod suspended under F-4B 153061. One of the rockets fired and zoomed across the deck to hit a Skyhawk's fuel tank, causing a chain reaction of explosions and fire on the flight deck. The aircraft on the deck were soon well ablaze, the fire fed by over 40,000 gallons of aviation fuel together with bombs and other ordnance. Bombs detonated blowing holes in the armoured deck through which fell burning fuel and ordnance that set fire to six lower decks. After the inferno was eventually brought under control the next day, a total of 134 men were dead, sixty-two more injured and twenty-one aircraft destroyed with another thirty-four damaged. (USN)

F-4B BuNo152987 of VF-151 'Fighting Vigilantes' armed with AIM-9D Sidewinder missiles taking off from the USS *Coral Sea*. The F-4B's relatively small weapons load was typical for *Coral Sea* due to the limited catapult capacity. This Phantom was part of a 'Rolling Thunder' strike on the Hải Dương railway bridge on 16 November 1967; It was leading the flak suppression flight at 12,000 feet on the way to the target when suddenly four SAMs shot up through the overcast below the formation. Although the pilot had started evasive manoeuvres, it was too late and his Phantom was hit by an SA-2 which riddled the F-4 with shrapnel all along its port side, causing a fire and engine failure. Seconds later, the entire tail unit disintegrated and the crew ejected, landing near Vĩnh Ninh, 14 miles south-east of their target. Both crew were captured and imprisoned until their release on 14 March 1973. On 24 March 1986 the 'Fighting Vigilantes' and VF-161 'Chargers', the last active duty carrier-based squadrons, were launched from *Midway* for the last time. The last Phantoms in reserve service were replaced by F/A-18s in 1990-91. (USN)

Above: Two F-4B Phantoms BuNos153011 and 153017 of VF-213 'Black Lions' from the USS *Kitty Hawk* in the Gulf of Tonkin on 23 January 1968. Both aircraft are carrying ten Mk.82 Slick 500lb General Purpose bombs, two AIM-7 Sparrow and two AIM-9 Sidewinder missiles and a centreline drop tank. Note the newly introduced fin-flip antennas. 153011 was upgraded to F-4N and later converted to QF-4N as '144'. It was expended on 19 August 2004. 153017 was also upgraded to F-4N and was SOC on 13 October 1983. It was salvaged at NAS North Island, California in 1984. (USN)

Opposite above: F-4B BuNo153018 of VF-114 'Aardvarks' armed with 'Sparrows' and 'Sidewinders' flying from the USS *Kitty Hawk* over the Gulf of Tonkin in March 1968. (The tail logo was borrowed from the 'BC' comic strip). On 13 March 1969, this Phantom was on a CAP (Combat Air Patrol) mission when the pilot discovered that his left throttle was stuck at 100 per cent. Eventually the port engine flamed out and the aircraft became uncontrollable, forcing the crew to eject before it crashed into the Gulf of Tonkin. (USN)

Opposite below: F-4B BuNo149445 of VF-142 'Ghost Riders' launching from USS *Constellation* in 1968 for a mission over Viêtnam. The 'Ghost Riders' were assigned to Carrier Air Wing 14 (CVW-14) aboard the 'Connie' for a deployment to Viêtnam from 29 May 1968 to 31 January 1969. This Phantom went to MASDC (as 8F0014) on 29 December 1971 and was salvaged by Allied Aircraft in August 1980. (USN)

NH
3018
VF-114
NAVY
205

NK
9445
VF-142
NAVY

Above: F-4B BuNo153020 of Fighter Squadron VF-92 'Silver Kings' approaches the aircraft carrier USS *Enterprise* in 1968. VF-92 was assigned to Carrier Air Wing 9 (CVW-9) aboard the 'Big E' for a deployment to Viêtnam from 3 January to 18 July 1968. On 23 May 1972, BuNo153020, flown by Lieutenant Commander R. E. McKeown and his back-seater, Lieutenant John Clyde Ensch, was credited with shooting down two MiG-17s over North Viêtnam. While with VF-161 'Chargers', CVW-5 aboard USS *Midway*, this Phantom was shot down by a Viêtnamese SA-2 surface-to-air missile near Namh Định at dusk on 25 August 1972. Lieutenant Commander Michael 'Ratso' Doyle and Ensch, who was badly injured, was taken into captivity. (USN)

Opposite above: F-4B BuNo153006 of VF-154 'Black Knights' from the USS *Ranger* dropping bombs in Viêtnam in February 1968. This Phantom was later converted to F-4N and it went to MASDC as 8F0092 on 5 November 1981 before being sent to Hill AFB, Utah in April 1985. (USN)

Opposite below: F-4B of VMFA(AW)-323 'Death Rattlers' Marine All Weather Fighter Attack Squadron at Đà Nẵng Air Base in 1968. The 'Death Rattlers' deployed to Đà Nẵng beginning on 25 October 1965 and combat operations started the day after they arrived. The squadron lost its first aircraft a week after they arrived when the squadron's executive officer was shot down by a SAM missile over North Viêtnam. It was the only Marine F-4 downed by a SAM during the war. 323 remained in Viêtnam until 1969, flying combat sorties from Đà Nẵng and Chu Lai. (USMC)

NE
3006
USS RANGER
NAVY
401

Above: F-4J BuNo153905 and F-4J 155854 of VF-84 'Jolly Rogers' from the USS *Franklin D. Roosevelt* over the Caribbean in August 1969. On 8 April 1973, BuNo153905, then with Marine Fighter Attack Training Squadron VMFAT-201 at NAS Pensacola, crashed. Captain R. E. McClane and First Lieutenant J. D. Chesney both ejected safely. (USN)

Opposie above: F-4J BuNo153909 of VF-84 'Jolly Rogers' taking off from the USS *Independence* in 1969. The 'Jolly Rogers' were assigned to Carrier Air Wing 7 (CVW-7) aboard the *Independence* for a deployment to the Mediterranean from 30 April 1968 to 27 January 1969. Upgraded to F-4S, BuNo153909 was sent to storage at NAD Cherry Point, North Carolina in April 1989, finally being SOC on 21 January 2003. (USN)

Opposite below: Eighteen months after the *Forrestal* fire in July 1967, a similar accident happened to the *Enterprise* as it worked up off Hawaii in preparation for a return to SE Asia on 14 January 1969. The carrier caught fire when a Zuni rocket on a Phantom ignited, causing a series of explosions on the flight deck that killed twenty-eight men and destroyed fifteen aircraft. In the foreground is F-4J BuNo153807 of VF-96 'Fighting Falcons' which went to MASDC (as 8F0188) on 29 March 1985. (USN)

3909
VF-84
NAVY
205

Above: F-4J BuNo155814 of VF-121 'Pacemakers'. This Phantom later served with VFMA-232 during which time it crashed near San Diego, California on 14 September 1970. Rebuilt as an F-4S, it was converted to a QF-4S drone, being expended on 24 March 2003. (USN)

Opposite above: F-4J of VF-21 'Freelancers' launching a radar-guided AIM-7 'Sparrow' missile in 1970. On 17 June 1965 Commander Louis Page and Lieutenant John Smith destroyed a MiG-17 with a 'Sparrow' and moments later, Lieutenant Jack Batson Jr. and Lieutenant Commander Robert Doremus destroyed another MiG-17 with an AIM-7. The 'Freelancers' made six further deployments to the war zone aboard USS *Coral Sea* and USS *Ranger* between 1966 and 1973. In 1968 the 'Freelancers' upgraded to the F-4J and continued to operate this model until 1979. The AIM-7D was produced between 1959 and 1962 and was capable of head-on intercepts. It was replaced in 1963 by the longer-ranged AIM-7E. (USN)

Opposite below: F-4J BuNo157292 of VF-84 'Jolly Rogers' on USS *Franklin D. Roosevelt* in 1970. This Phantom was later converted to F-4S, finally going to AMARC (as 8F0245) in November 1986.

NE

7292
VF-84
NAVY
202

Above: F-4J of VF-96 'Fighting Falcons' landing on the USS *America* in 1970. Several F-4s of VF-96 were destroyed during the USS *Enterprise* fire on 14 January 1969. VF-96 embarked aboard the USS *America* for a deployment to Viêtnam from 10 April to 21 December 1970. (USN)

Opposite above: F-4J BuNos155562 and 155864 of VF-84 'Jolly Rogers' on USS *Franklin D. Roosevelt* in 1970. 155562 was converted to F-4S and while with VMFA-251 'Thunderbolts', it crashed on Chocolate Mountain Range, California on 2 September 1979. 155864 was later upgraded to F-4S and was WFU at MCAS Cherry Point, North Carolina in November 1991. Converted to a QF-4S drone ('112'), it was expended on 21 December 2000. (USN)

Opposite below: A Soviet frigate shadows the USS *Independence* in the Mediterranean in 1970. On deck are F-4Js of VF-33 'Tarsiers' (EG) and VF-84 'Jolly Rogers' (AG). BuNo155544 in the foreground was upgraded to F-4S and later converted to a QF-4S drone. It was expended in a missile test on 29 March 2004. (USN)

VF-84
5562
207
NAVY

AG
USS INDEPENDENCE
207
5544

Above: F-4J 153837 of Det 66, VF-101 'Grim Reapers' from the USS *America* in flight in 1971. Whilst with VF-101 on 25 August 1975, this Phantom crashed on approach to the USS *Franklin D. Roosevelt*. (USN)

Opposite above: A Soviet Tu-95 'Bear' is joined by a pair of VF-213 'Black Lions' F-4J Phantom escorts assigned to Attack Carrier Air Wing 11 (CVW-11) in the USS *Kitty Hawk* while en route from San Diego, California to the Philippines on 5 July 1971. (USN)

Opposite below: F-4J BuNo157270 'CAG Bird' of VF-114 'Aardvarks' about to launch from the USS *Kitty Hawk* during the deployment to Viêtnam between 6 November 1970 and 17 July 1971. The aircraft was the personalised Phantom of the Commander Air Group (CAG) of Attack Carrier Air Wing Eleven (CVW-11). (Note the differently coloured stars on the tail fin, which represent the different squadrons of CVW-11). An F-4J of VF-213 'Black Lions' is also visible. On 28 March 1978 with VMFA-212 'Lancers', BuNo157270 was written off at MCAS Kaneohe Bay, Hawaii.

NH
NAVY

Above: F-4J 154784 of VMFA-333 'Shamrocks', which was shot down by a SAM over North Viêtnam on 11 September 1972 shortly after shooting down a MiG-21. Major Lee T. 'The Bear' Lasseter, the 38-year-old Squadron Executive Officer and his RIO, Captain 'L'il' John D. Cummings (both 'Top Gun' graduates) ejected and were picked up by SAR helicopters. It was the only all-Marine Corps MiG kill of the war. Marine F-4 pilots claimed three MiGs (two while on exchange duty with the USAF) at the cost of seventy-five aircraft lost in combat, mostly to ground fire and four in accidents. (USMC)

Opposite above: F-4B of VF-14 'Tophatters' intercepting an Egyptian Tupolev Tu-16 Badger bomber. VF-14 was assigned to Attack Carrier Air Wing 1 (CVW-1) aboard the aircraft carrier USS *John F. Kennedy* for a deployment to the Mediterranean Sea from 18 November 1971 to 10 May 1972. (USN)

Opposite below: F-4J BuNo155769 of VF-96 'Fighting Falcons' on the elevator aboard the USS *Constellation* in 1972. VF-96 was assigned to Carrier Air Wing 9 (CVW-9) aboard *Constellation* for a deployment to Viêtnam from 1 October 1971 to 1 July 1972. Converted to F-4S and issued to VF-302 'Stallions', BuNo155769 crashed during a rainstorm on 4 April 1983 during landing roll-out at NAS Dallas, Texas, Lieutenant Commander C. J. Tinker and Lieutenant J. L. Walsh ejecting safely. (USN)

RB
NAVY

NG
06
USS CONSTELLATION
5769
VF-96
NAVY
06
00
NG
TION
5799
155799
VF-92

Above: Phantoms and A-7 Corsairs aboard the USS *John F. Kennedy* in the Mediterranean in 1972. From 14-28 September 1972, *John F. Kennedy* participated in NATO Exercise 'Strong Express'. (USN)

Opposite above: KA-6D of VA-85 'Black Falcons' refuelling F-4B Bu151420 of VF-11 'Red Rippers' from the USS *Forrestal* in 1972. With VMFA-321 'Hell's Angels', Bu151420 overshot the runway at NAS Whidbey Island and ended up with its nose in Puget Sound. It was written off in a ground accident at NAS North Island, California on 16 January 1976. (USN)

Opposite below: F-4Js of VMFA-232 'Red Devils' and A-6 Intruders at Nam Phong in 1972. BuNo155822 was later converted to F-4S and it went to AMARC (as 8F0306) on 23 August 1988. (USN)

1420
VF-11
NAVY
110
149945
NAVY
523

WT
5822
VMFA-232
MARINES
18
19

Above: In January 1969, seven modified F-4Js were assigned to the USN's 'Blue Angels' demonstration team. The team made its debut with the type at MCAS Yuma, Arizona on 15 March 1969 and for five seasons, thrilled millions worldwide with its precision F-4 flying. The 'Blues' flew the F-4J until the end of the 1973 season, when the energy crisis forced a change to the A-4F Skyhawk. (McDonnell Douglas)

Opposite above: AIM-7 Sparrow and AIM-9 Sidewinder-armed F-4B BuNo153045 of VF-114 'Aardvarks' from the USS *Kitty Hawk* in the Gulf of Tonkin in March 1968. Later upgraded to F-4N, BuNo153045 was SOC on 7 September 1983. (USN)

Opposite below: F-4J BuNo155787 of VF-96 'Fighting Falcons' of the USS *Constellation* on the cat ready for launch in the Gulf of Tonkin in May 1972 during the deployment to Viêtnam from 1 October 1971 to 1 July 1972. VF-96 embarked aboard the USS *Ranger* for the first deployment to Viêtnam (5 August 1964 to 6 May 1965); the USS *Enterprise* (26 October 1965 to 21 June 1966) and the USS *America* (10 April to 21 December 1970). Converted to F-4S, BuNo155787 went to AMARC (as 8F0285) on 9 June 1987. (USN)

NH
3045
VF-114
NAVY
211

04
NG
5787
USS CONSTELLATION
155787
VF-96
NAVY
104

U.S. AIR FORCE
17955
3783
VX4
NAVY

NG
5895
USS CONSTELLATION
114

Above: F-4Bs BuNos150476 and 152252 of VMFA-531 'Gray Ghosts' on the USS *Forrestal* in 1973. 150476 was later converted to F-4N and while with VF-202 'Superheats' on 14 May 1983, it crashed near Comanche, Texas. BuNo152252 was also upgraded to F-4N. It was written off on 23 August 1982 while with VF-154 'Black Knights' on the USS *Coral Sea*. (USN)

Opposite above: F-4J BuNo153783 'Playboy Black Bunny' of VX-4 at NAS Point Mugu, California and SR-71A 'Blackbird' 61-7955 (which is now on display at the Air Force Flight Test Center Museum at Edwards AFB, California) in 1973. This colourful Phantom (the first of two VX-4 'The Evaluators' to wear this livery) went to AMARC (as 8F0097) before being flown out to San Diego on 30 November 1983 for NARF (Naval Air Rework Facility), making its first flight on 18 March 1967. The RAF acquired the 'Playboy Black Bunny' on 30 August 1984 (re-serialled ZE352) and it ended service as a battle damage repair trainer at Laarbruch (9086M) until WFU on 26 February 1991. (USN)

Opposite below: F-4J BuNo155895 of VF-96 'Fighting Falcons', part of Carrier Air Wing Nine (CVW-9) on the USS *Constellation* (visible in the background). The aircraft is fully armed with radar-guided AIM-7 'Sparrow' and AIM-9 'Sidewinder' missiles, indicating that this photo was probably taken during the deployment to Viêtnam between 1971 and 1974. VF-96 embarked on the 'Connie' for its final Viêtnam cruise from 5 January to 11 October 1973. Between 21 June and 23 December 1974, the 'Fighting Falcons' along with sister squadron VF-92 'Silver Kings' made its last operational deployment with CVW-9, aboard *Constellation*, before being disestablished on 1 December 1975. While with VF-213 'Black Lions', BuNo155895 crashed on 19 November 1974. (USN)

Above: F-4J BuNo153827 of VF-92 'Silver Kings' from the *Constellation* in 1973. Later converted to F-4S, it finished its service career when it went to AMARC (as 8F0214) on 28 April 1986. (USN)

Opposite above: F-4J BuNo157257 of VF-114 'Aardvarks' assigned to Carrier Air Wing 11 (CVW-11) for a deployment to the Western Pacific from 21 May to 15 December 1975 intercepting Soviet Tu-16 'Badger'. This Phantom was converted to F-4S, finally ending its service at MASDC (as 8F0178) on 26 December 1984. (USN)

Opposite below: F-4J BuNo153804 of VF-213 'Black Lions' on the cat of USS *Kitty Hawk* in 1975. It later served with VMFA-122 'Crusaders' and may have been written off on 21 December 1977. (USN)

NH
7257
NA
104

200
NH
3804

Above: Over the Mediterranean in April 1977, F-4N BuNo152970 of VF-51 'Screaming Eagles' intercepts a Soviet-built Tu-22 'Blinder' bomber and maritime attack aircraft being delivered to Libya. This Phantom was converted to F-4N and on 14 October 1983, it went to MASDC (as 8F0125). Converted to a QF-4N drone 'as 143 and 36', it was expended in a missile test on 26 June 2001. (USN)

Opposite above: F-4N BuNo151008 of VF-111 'Sundowners' launching from the USS *Franklin D Roosevelt* in February 1977. VF-111 was assigned to Carrier Air Wing 19 (CVW-19) for FDR's final cruise to the Mediterranean Sea from 4 October 1976 to 21 April 1977. *Franklin D. Roosevelt* was decommissioned on 30 September 1977. BuNo151008 crashed while with VF-171 'Aces' on 20 November 1978. (USN)

Opposite below: F-4J BuNo155572 of VF-121 'Pacemakers' landing at NAS Miramar in 1978. This Phantom was upgraded to F-4S and was WFU at MCAS Cherry Point, North Carolina in April 1989. Converted to a QF-4S drone, it was expended on 21 November 2003.

NM
03
1008
151008
VF-111
USS ROOSEVELT
NAVY
203

152
NJ
52
5572
VF-121

Above: F-4B BuNo152318 of VMFA-323 'Death Rattlers' on the *Coral Sea* in 1979-80. VMFA-323 embarked on its only aircraft carrier cruise in the F-4 Phantom in November 1979. After liberty stops in Korea, Thailand and Singapore, the *Coral Sea* arrived in the Arabian Sea in January 1980 flying protection caps for itself and USS *Nimitz*. On 24 April 1980, VMFA-323 was prepared to fly combat missions into southern Iran in support of a US hostages rescue attempt in Operation 'Eagle Claw', with the mission to shoot down any Iranian combat aircraft that attempted to take off. When 'Eagle Claw' failed, VMFA-323 F-4s flew missions around the clock until all US support ships had exited the Persian Gulf and Gulf of Oman. Converted to F-4N, BuNo152318 went to MASDC (as 8F0132) on 19 October 1983 and was salvaged in November 2004.

Opposite above: F-4B BuNo152241 of VF-114 'Aardvarks' (seen here with VMFA-323 'Death Rattlers' landing on the USS *Kitty Hawk*) crashed into the sea off USS *Oriskany* on 19 December 1979.

Opposite below: F-4J BuNo158363 of VF-21 'Freelancers' from the USS *Ranger* intercepting a Soviet Tu-95 over the Pacific in 1979. This Phantom went to MASDC (as 8F0187) on 28 March 1985.

NH
2241
NAVY

NE
USS RANGER
8363
VF-21
NAVY
203

F-4Ns of VMFA-323 'Death Rattlers' from the USS *Coral Sea* in 1979. 151011 was temporarily loaned to the USAF as 62-12191. Returned, it was upgraded to F-4N, finally being SOC on 16 June 1982 and was assigned as a ground training aircraft at NAS Alameda, California. 153008 was also converted to F-4N, going to MASDC on 19 October 1982, later being assigned as a battle damage repair trainer at RAF Alconbury, England in May 1986. BuNo150628 is preserved on the USS *Intrepid* at the Sea-Air-Space Museum in New York. It was one of the Phantoms that flew top cover during Operation 'Eagle Claw', a joint USAF/USMC attempt to rescue fifty-two diplomats held captive at the US Embassy in Tehran on 24 April 1980 which ended in disaster. BuNo150480 was temporarily loaned to the USAF as 62-12170 and when it returned, it was upgraded to F-4N. It was SOC on 2 March 1983.

The scene on the flight deck of the USS *Coral Sea* in 1979 with Phantoms of VMFA-323 'Death Rattlers' and VMFA-531 'Gray Ghosts', Corsairs and A-6 Intruders ranged on the forward deck. BuNo153016 was later upgraded to F-4N and was written off on 12 January 1983 while with VF-21 'Freelancers' on the USS *Coral Sea* and was WFU in April 1983. Initially preserved at San Diego, California, it was part of the Champlin Fighter Collection at Falcon Field, Mesa, Arizona until this museum went out of business; this Phantom is now at CAF Arizona Wing Museum at Falcon Field, Mesa on loan from the National Naval Aviation Museum.

Above: F-4J BuNo155839 and 155847 of VFMA-212 'Lancers' being refuelled by KC-130R of VMGR-352 near Hawaii on 2 October 1979. BuNo155839 was converted to F-4S and went to AMARC as 8F0250 on 12 December 1986. BuNo155847 was also upgraded to F-4S, being WFU at MCAS Cherry Point, North Carolina and converted to a QF-4S drone; this was the last QF-4S to be converted for the USN under its drone programme. On 3 March 2003 this aircraft left for NAWS Point Mugu, California where it was expended on 19 November 2003 after crashing on San Nicholas Island, California.

Opposite above: F-4J BuNo155813 of VF-96 'Fighting Falcons' from the USS *Constellation*, seen here refuelling from a Grumman KA-6D in-flight refuelling tanker, was later converted to F-4S. While with VMFAT-101 (Marine Fighter Attack Training Squadron 101 - 'the Sharpshooters') on 11 December 1984, it crashed shortly after take-off from MCAS Yuma, Arizona killing one crew member. BuNo155569 at the top of the picture, which served with VF-92 'Silver Kings' in the early 1970s, was written off on 31 July 1980 when it too was serving with VMFAT-101.

Opposite below: A typically crowded carrier deck scene with BuNo157275 of VF-84 'Jolly Rogers' in the foreground. On 13 April 1980 while with VF-103 'Sluggers' on the *Saratoga*, this Phantom crashed into the Mediterranean. Lieutenant J. G. Carlton and Lieutenant (j.g.) R. Ritorto both ejected safely.

NG
556
NG
NAVY

AE
7275
VF-84
205
202
602

Above: F-4S BuNo155749, which is credited with a MiG-17 kill on 10 May 1972 with VF-96 'Fighting Falcons', is seen at NAS Whiting Field in 1982 in the markings of VMFA-235 'Death Angels'. In 1972, the period 10 May to 15 October produced all five American aces (three USAF and two USN) of the Việtnam War. There was intense rivalry between the two services, not least in the 'ace' stakes. On 10 May, Navy fighters destroyed eight MiGs, six by F-4J Phantoms of VF-96 'Fighting Falcons' on USS *Constellation*. Lieutenant 'Randy' Cunningham and Lieutenant (j.g.) William 'Irish' Driscoll, his RIO became the first American aircrew to qualify as aces solely as a result of action in Việtnam when they shot down their third, fourth and fifth MiGs before their F-4J ('ShowTime 100') was hit by a SAM and went down off the coast. Cunningham and Driscoll were rescued by a helicopter from the *Okinawa* and returned uninjured to the *Constellation* to a hero's welcome and to share their victories with their colleagues. Converted to a QF-4S drone, 155749 crashed at Point Mugu Air Show on 20 April 2002. Both crew ejected, but hit the ground before their chutes could open and they were killed.

Opposite above: F-4J BuNo153769 of VF-31 'Tomcatters' at a snowy Oceana on 11 February 1980 sporting a red star denoting a MiG 'kill' after three tries with AIM-9 Sidewinders. VF-31 'Tomcatters' Commander Samuel C. Flynn and Lieutenant William H. John destroyed a MiG-21 with an AIM-9 on 21 June 1972 but it was with 157307. At the time of this photo, Commander Flynn was assigned 101 so it reflects his kill.

Opposite below: F-4S of VF-74 'Bedevilers' from the USS *Forrestal* intercepts a Soviet Tupolev Tu-95 'Bear D' about 70 kilometres off the coast of Virginia in 1982. The F-4S was escorting the Cuba-based Tu-95, which had just penetrated the US air defence zone to aerially view sea trials of the (then) new nuclear-powered aircraft carrier USS *Carl Vinson* on 26 January 1982. VF-74 made their final cruise with the F-4 from May to 16 November 1982. In February 1983 they began the transition to the F-14 Tomcat.

CHAPTER 2

USAF

In USAF service, the F-4 was initially designated the F-110 Spectre prior to the introduction of the 1962 United States Tri-Service aircraft designation system. The USAF quickly embraced the design and became the largest Phantom user. Unlike the Navy and Marine Corps, which flew the Phantom with a Naval Aviator (pilot) in the front seat and a Naval Flight Officer as a radar intercept officer (RIO) in the back seat, the USAF initially flew its Phantoms with a rated Air Force Pilot in front and back seats. While the rear pilot (GIB or 'guy in back') could fly and ostensibly land the aircraft, he had fewer flight instruments and a very restricted forward view. The Air Force later assigned a rated Air Force Navigator qualified as a weapon/targeting systems officer (later designated as weapon systems officer or WSO) in the rear seat instead of another pilot. However, all USAF Phantoms retained dual flight controls throughout their service life.

The first USAF Phantoms in Viêtnam were F-4Cs from the 555th Tactical Fighter Squadron 'Triple Nickle', which arrived in December 1964. On 10 July 1965, F-4Cs of the 45th Tactical Fighter Squadron, 15th TFW on temporary assignment in Ubon, Thailand scored the USAF's first victories against North Viêtnamese MiG-17s using AIM-9 Sidewinder air-to-air missiles. On 26 April 1966, an F-4C from the 480th Tactical Fighter Squadron scored the first aerial victory by a US aircrew over a North Viêtnamese MiG-21. On 24 July 1965, another Phantom from the 45th Tactical Fighter Squadron became the first American aircraft to be downed by an enemy SAM. On 5 October 1966, an 8th Tactical Fighter Wing F-4C became the first US jet lost to an air-to-air missile, fired by a MiG-21. Early aircraft suffered from leaks in wing fuel tanks that required re-sealing after each flight and eighty-five aircraft were found to have cracks in outer wing ribs and stringers. There were also problems with aileron control cylinders, electrical connectors and engine compartment fires. RF-4Cs made their debut in Viêtnam on 30 October 1965, flying the hazardous post-strike reconnaissance missions.

Although the F-4C was essentially identical to the Navy/Marine Corps F-4B in flight performance and carried the AIM-9 Sidewinder missiles, USAF F-4Ds initially arrived in June 1967 equipped with AIM-4 Falcons. (Produced in both heat-seeking and radar-guided versions, the AIM-4 Falcon was designed to shoot down slow bombers with limited manoeuvrability but it was ineffective against manoeuvrable fighters in Viêtnam. Lacking proximity fusing, the missile would only detonate if a direct hit was scored. With the AIM-4's poor kill record rendering the USAF F-4 ineffective at air-to-air combat, the fighters were instead modified to carry the USN-designed AIM-9 Sidewinder missile, which was already carried on USN and USMC F-4 and F-8 Crusader jet fighters.)

From the initial deployment of the F-4C to SE Asia, USAF Phantoms performed both air superiority and ground attack roles, supporting not only ground troops in South Viêtnam but also conducting bombing sorties in Laos and North Viêtnam. As the F-105 force underwent severe attrition between 1965 and 1968, the bombing role of the F-4 proportionately increased until after November 1970 (when the last F-105D was withdrawn from combat), it became the primary USAF tactical ordnance delivery system. Sixteen squadrons of Phantoms were permanently deployed between 1965 and 1973, and seventeen others were deployed on temporary combat assignments. Peak numbers of combat F-4s occurred in 1972 when 353 were based in Thailand. A total of 442 Air Force Phantom fighter-bombers were lost, 370 in combat and 193 of those over North Viêtnam (thirty-three to MiGs, thirty to SAMs, 307 to AAA and nine were destroyed on the ground by VC action while 63 were lost in operational accidents). USAF F-4C/D/E crews scored 107½ MiG kills in SE Asia - fifty by radar-guided AIM-7 'Sparrow', thirty-one by heart-seeking AIM-9 'Sidewinder', five by AIM-4 'Falcon', 15½ by gun and six by other means. On 2 June 1972, a Phantom flying at supersonic speed shot down a MiG-19 over Thud Ridge in Viêtnam for the first supersonic gun kill. At a recorded speed of Mach 1.2, Major Phil Handley's shoot down was the first and only recorded gun kill while flying at supersonic speeds.

In October 1972, the first squadron of EF-4C 'Wild Weasel' aircraft deployed to Thailand on temporary duty. The 'E' prefix was later dropped and the aircraft was simply known as the F-4C 'Wild Weasel'. The RF-4C was operated by four squadrons and of the eighty-three losses, seventy-two were in combat including thirty-eight over North Viêtnam (seven to SAMs and sixty-five to AAA). By war's end, the US Air Force had lost a total of 528 F-4 and RF-4C Phantoms. When combined with US Navy and Marine Corps losses of 233 Phantoms, 761 F-4/RF-4 Phantoms were lost in the Viêtnam War. The F-4G 'Wild Weasel' was a modified F-4E with highly sophisticated electronic warfare systems for defence-suppression purposes, and was an interim version of the sophisticated F-4J for the USN. Its development began in 1963.

Phantoms would eventually equip numerous tactical fighter and tactical reconnaissance units in the USAF active, National Guard and Air Force Reserve. In the Air National Guard, F-4Cs entered service with the 170th Tactical Fighter Squadron/183rd Tactical Fighter Group, Illinois ANG in January 1972 when they became the first Guard unit to transition to Phantoms from Republic F-84F Thunderstreaks, which were found to have corrosion problems. The last F-4Cs were phased out by the 123rd FIS, Oregon ANG in October 1989. F-4Ds, which first went to North Dakota's 178th FIS in March 1977, were retired by the 184th TFG, Kansas ANG in March 1990. F-4Es initially equipped Missouri's 110th TFS and New Jersey's 141st TFS during the summer of 1985. During 1991, the last F-4Es were phased out but a version new to the Guard, the F-4G 'Wild Weasel', entered ANG service with the 190th TFS in Idaho. All ANG F-4s had been replaced by the end of 1996.

It was not until October 1980 that AFRES became a Phantom operator when the 915th Airborne Early Warning and Control Group at Homestead AFB, Florida was redesignated as the 915th Tactical Fighter Group (TFG) and F-4Cs were assigned to the 93rd TFS. By 1984, F-4Ds had been delivered to four more squadrons and the 93rd TFS had also been re-equipped with F-4Ds. In 1988, the 457th TFS at Carswell AFB, Texas began receiving F-4Es and in 1989, the 93rd TFS became the first AFRES squadron to replace its Phantoms with F-16A/Bs. Conversion of the remaining four F-4 squadrons to F-16s was completed by 1991.

On 15 August 1990, twenty-four F-4G 'Wild Weasel V's and six RF-4Cs were deployed to Shaikh Isa AB, Bahrain for Operation 'Desert Storm'. The F-4G was the only aircraft in the USAF inventory equipped for the Suppression of Enemy Air Defences (SEAD) role and was needed to protect coalition aircraft from Iraq's extensive air defence system. The final flight of an Air Force QF-4 from Tyndall AFB took place on 27 May 2015 to Holloman AFB. After Tyndall AFB ceased operations, the 53rd Weapons Evaluation Group at Holloman became the fleet of twenty-two QF-4s' last remaining operator, with the final unmanned flight taking place in August 2016. The type was officially retired from US military service with a four-ship flight at Holloman during an event on 21 December 2016. The remaining QF-4s were demilitarised after 1 January 2017.

F-4C's 63-7412 and 63-7688 of the 57th FIS 'Black Knights' at Keflavik NAS, Iceland and a FG.1 on 43 Squadron at RAF Leuchars in Scotland shadowing a 'Bear' in the Northern Atlantic. 43 Squadron reformed at Leuchars on 1 September 1969 in the air defence role with the Phantom which it flew until its replacement by the Tornado F.3 in September 1989. The first F-4C was assigned to the 57th FIS on 16 April 1973, as TAC was replacing its F-4Cs with F-4E models at the end of the Viêtnam War. By 30 June the squadron had six F-4Cs and additional F-4Cs were received in the third quarter of 1974. The last of the F-102s were replaced in early 1975 when additional F-4Cs were received from TAC squadrons at Luke AFB and George AFB, the last F-4C arriving in March 1976. Robert M. Sihler, a F-4C Weapons System Officer in the 57th FIS, recalled a standard intercept of a 'Bear' by two F-4s after the alert crews were activated: 'In June 1973 we probably averaged two intercepts of 'Bears' per week. They were the only aircraft we saw while I was there. Generally, the intercepts occurred on Fridays and Sundays, as the 'Bears' flew from Murmansk to Cuba on training and, we guessed, 'fun' missions. Generally, we did these barrel rolls at the request of the Soviet crew members. They gave us hand signals to let us know they wanted us to do it. They photographed us as well. The Cold War was winding down and the attitudes on both sides had improved.' 7412 finished its service career as a battle damage repair trainer at Cannon AB, New Mexico and was scrapped on 1 October 1988. 63-7688 went to AMARC (as FP047) on 19 March 1987 and was then sent to be a target on the Tolicha Peak Range in Nevada in March 1991. (Robert M. Sihler/The *Aviationist*)

RF-4C 64-1054 of the 16th TRS, 60th TRW in Viêtnam in 1965. On 30 October 1965, nine RF-4C all-weather, day-night, high-low reconnaissance Phantoms from the 16th TRS were deployed on a TDY basis to Tan Son Nhut AB, Republic of South Viêtnam. They were operated for eight years, starting on 31 October 1965, by the 11th, 12th, 14th and 16th TRSs from Tan Son Nhut and from Udorn RTAFB. By November 1970 the RF-4C had completely replaced the RF-101Cs. Altogether, 503 RF-4Cs were delivered to the Air Force between May 1964 and January 1974, eighty-three of them being lost during the Viêtnam War, seven falling victim to SAMs, sixty-five to AAA or small arms fire, four being destroyed on the ground and seven to operational accidents. In 1965 the first Phantoms were introduced to Europe when the RF-4C began arriving at the 10th TRW Wing at RAF Alconbury on 12 May and the first F-4C arrived at the 81st TFW at RAF Bentwaters on 4 October. 64-1054 was hit in the rear fuselage by AAA near Cao Mại/Đồng Hới in the north central coast of North Viêtnam during a night reconnaissance mission on 19/20 August 1966. The aircraft crashed almost immediately and although Captain E. T. Hawks ejected and was rescued about six hours later by a Navy helicopter, his navigator, 1st Lieutenant Richard M. Milikin was killed. (USAF)

The Phantom's greatest claim to fame was in the Viêtnam War of 1965-73 (here a USAF Phantom makes a rocket attack on a target in Viêtnam in 1966) where they became most famous for their MiG kills, ground-attack missions, suppression of enemy air defences (SEAD) sorties and attacks on bridges with 'dumb' and later 'smart' bombs. The first USAF Phantoms in South-East Asia were the F-4Cs of the 45th TFS, which were sent to Ubon in April 1965. On 9 June 1965, the first operational (non-combat) loss of an F-4 in SE Asia occurred when 64-0674 in the 45th TFS, 15th TFW ran out of fuel after a strike in South Viêtnam. On 20 June the first Phantom combat loss occurred when a 45th TFS F-4C (64-0685) was downed by a MiG-17. Phantoms and MiGs met each other over Viêtnam on many occasions throughout the first half of 1967 and American crews also continued to run the gauntlet of SAMs and ground fire. (USAF)

US Air Force ground personnel prepare AIM-7E 'Sparrow' missiles for loading on F-4C 63-7473 and 64-0830 in the 559th Tactical Fighter Squadron, 12th Tactical Fighter Wing at Cam Ran Air Base in South Viêtnam in 1967. 63-7473, which is not equipped with the IR-sensor, is armed with a 20 mm gun pod and napalm canisters. It went to AMARC (as FP059) on 27 April 1987 and became a target on the Tonicha Peak Range, Nevada in April 1991. 64-0830 crashed in Laos on 22 March 1968 following a bomb malfunction over Khe Sanh. One crew member was captured, the other was reported missing. The Phantom (and the F-105 Thunderchief) was tasked with strategic bombing in North Viêtnam but neither fighter had been designed for this mission, being handicapped by the limitations of their radar-guided AIM-7 Sparrow and heat-seeking AIM-9 Sidewinder missile armament, neither of which had been designed for fighter versus fighter combat. The great advantage conferred by the 'Sparrow' - its ability to engage the enemy from any angle at up to twelve miles - was nullified by a rule of engagement which called for visual identification of the enemy before firing. The Sidewinder could be fired from up to one mile, but only from the rear, in a 30° cone that led to the engine's heat. Both missiles were limited by their reaction to g-forces and both required a set-up time that was difficult to effect in air combat. (USAF)

F-4D 66-7733 in the 480th Tactical Fighter Squadron at Phú Cat AB in 1969. This Phantom was expended on 11 October 1972 when it was launched from Vandenberg AFB. In May 1967, F-4Ds of the 555th TFS were sent to Viêtnam. This version, developed from the F-4C, introduced improved weapons delivery systems. The type flew for the first time on 7 December 1965 and began equipping the USAF in March 1966. On 22 March 1966, the first F-4D arrived at the 36th TFW, Bitburg. F-4D crews scored twenty-six victories with Sparrows, 6½ with gunfire, five each with Sidewinders and Falcons, and two while manoeuvring. In South-East Asia, a total of eighty-three RF-4Cs were lost. (USAF)

F-4C of 557th Tactical Fighter Squadron, 12th Tactical Fighter Wing at Cam Ranh Bay AB, delivers close air support to armoured vehicles in South Viêtnam during April 1969. (USAF)

F-4C 63-7544 (nearest the camera) and F-4C 63-7414 (behind) fully loaded with 750 lb general purpose bombs and rockets refuelling from a KC-135 before making a strike against Communist targets in North Viêtnam. While with the 366th TFW on 9 December 1966, 63-7544 was shot down by friendly fire near Đà Nẵng Air Base. The crew ejected safely. 63-7414 was retired from flying duties in 1986 and was used for Bomb Damage Repair (BDR) at RAF Woodbridge before being transported to the Midland Air Museum, Coventry, England where it has been in open-storage for years and still wears the faded markings of its last operator, the New York Air National Guard. The Phantom, which had also served with the 4453rd Combat Crew Training Wing, is unlikely ever to be restored. (USAF)

A LORAN-equipped F-4D (66-8776) from the 13th Tactical Fighter Squadron, 432nd Tactical Reconnaissance Wing leads two US Navy F-4Bs (BuNos151513 and 152258) of VF-151 'Vigilantes' during a bombing mission over Viêtnam in 1971. VF-151 was assigned to Carrier Air Wing 5 (CVW-5) aboard the aircraft carrier USS *Midway* for a deployment to Viêtnam from 16 April to 6 November 1971. Phantoms flew on bombing strikes in South-East Asia with a lead ship (because the F-4 was not normally equipped for accurate medium level bomb delivery) which signalled when to release the bomb load. While with the 23rd TFS, 52nd TFW on 7 December 1978, F-4D 66-8776 crashed near Solingen, West Germany on night training mission with a low cloud ceiling. The aircraft came out of the clouds and the aircrew ejected safely before the aircraft impacted the ground. BuNo152258 was upgraded to F-4N and converted to a QF-4N drone. While with VMFA-531 'Gray Ghosts' on 31 March 1982, the pilot of BuNo151513, 1st Lieutenant Michael J. Flood experienced G-induced loss-of-consciousness and his back-seater, 1st Lieutenant J. W. Williams ejected both himself and pilot before the Phantom crashed into the Pacific off California. (USAF)

Above: EF-4C in the 67th Tactical Fighter Squadron, 18th Tactical Fighter Wing over North Viêtnam in December 1972. It is armed with AGM-45 Shrike and AIM-7 Sparrow missiles and carries an AN/ALQ-72 ECM pod. The EF-4C 'Wild Weasel IV' was a parallel development with the F-105G 'Wild Weasel III' programme. Thirty-six aircraft F-4Cs were modified and fitted with the AN/APR-25 Radar Homing and Warning System (RHAWS), AN/APR-26 SAM launch warning system and ER-142 electronic counter-measures receiver. After the F-4G became available in the late 1970s, these aircraft were flown as regular F-4Cs. (USAF)

Opposite above: A KC-135A refuels a SAM Hunter killer group of the 388th Tactical Fighter Wing at Korat en route to North Viêtnam for a strike during 'Operation Linebacker' in October 1972. The two F-4Es are from the 34th Tactical Fighter Squadron and the F-105G Thunderchief 'Wild Weasel' aircraft are from the 17th TFS ('JB') and the 561st TFS ('WW'). F-4E 68-0309 went to the South Korean Air Force in November 1990 as 80-309. (USAF)

Opposite below: F-4E 68-0311 in the 388th Tactical Fighter Wing at Anderson AFB in 1972. The 'E' was sent to Viêtnam in November 1968. While with the 110th TFS, 131st Tactical Fighter Wing, Missouri ANG on 8 April 1990 during a routine training sortie over the practice range in Crawford County, 68-0311 veered off the runway at Lambert-Saint Louis Airport during take-off and the central fuel tank ruptured, bursting into flames. The WSO First Lieutenant Kevin W. Greeley received an uncommanded out-of-the-envelope ejection and was severely injured. The pilot ejection seat did not fire but Captain Carl Arizpe was uninjured. (USAF)

U.S. AIR FORCE

Above: The USAF 'Thunderbirds', seen over the Hawaiian kune hai in 1971, only used the F-4E for four seasons from 1969 to 1973 when they transitioned to the Northrop T-38 Talon after rising fuel costs forced a change of aircraft. The team transitioned from the North American F-100D Super Sabre to the F-4E in 1969, making their debut at the Air Force Academy in Colorado Springs on 4 June that year. Changes to the show routine were required to keep the performance close to show centre because the F-4Es were so much more powerful than the Team's previous mount. White polyurethane paint was adopted in order to give the F-4Es an appealing uniform colour. (USAF)

Opposite above: F-4C 63-7473 of the 34th Tactical Fighter Squadron at Hickam AFB, Hawaii in 1975. This Phantom went to AMARC (as FP059) on 27 April 1987 and later, in April 1991, was sent to be a target on Tonicha Peak Range, Nevada. (USAF)

Opposite below: RF-4C 65-0893 of the 106th TRS at Ramstein AB in Germany in 1976. This Phantom went to AMARC (as FP815) on 5 February 1992 and was still on the AMARC inventory in 2008. (USAF)

473

AF
65 893

Above: F4E 69-0283 of the 347th Tactical Fighter Wing taking off during Exercise 'Scarlet Duck' on 20 April 1977. It was later assigned to the 401st Tactical Fighter Wing at Torrejón, Madrid, Spain and was probably leased to the Imperial Iranian AF during September 1972 to January 1973, possibly as 3-688. It went to the 32nd TFS on 21 November 1974 and was converted to F-4G in 1979. On 12 January 1981 while serving with the 90th TFS, 3rd TFW it was written off at Clark AB, Philippines. (USAF)

Opposite above: F-4Cs 64-0851 and 64-0806 of the Hawaii ANG during a refuelling mission with a KC-135A in 1979. 64-0851 was SOC on 27 October 1986 and is preserved on a pole on University Avenue at the Tuskegee Institute in Macon, Alabama. It was flown by Colonel Daniel 'Chappie' James, Jr., Tuskegee University graduate and first Black Four-Star General in the US Armed Services, on his last combat mission - 'Operation Bolo' on 2 January 1967 - when the 8th Tactical Fighter Wing destroyed seven MiG-21s. The aircraft was donated to Tuskegee University by the US Air Force with the assistance of Air University at Maxwell Air Force Base, Alabama. 64-0806, which was SOC on 7 August 1987, is preserved at Nellis AFB, Nevada. (USAF)

Opposite below: F-4C 64-0793 of the 199th Tactical Fighter Squadron, 154th Composite Group, Hawaii Air National Guard, being armed with AIM-9P 'Sidewinder' and AIM-7E 'Sparrow' missiles at Hickam Air Force Base, Hawaii on 21 March 1980. In October 1987 this Phantom was assigned as a battle damage repair trainer at Hickam AFB and it then went to AMARC (as FP815) on 5 February 1992. (USAF)

71496
806
AF
64 851

793

Above: F-4Es 66-0300 and 66-0370 of the 57th FIS at Keflavik, Iceland shadowing a Soviet Tu 95D 'Bear' on 28 September 1980. In early 1978, preparations for the exchange of the F-4C for F-4Es were underway with the first two aircraft landing on 21 March. Both Phantoms were sold to Turkey in 1987. An F-4 bearing the serial number is 66-0300 is today on outdoor display at Keflavik AB, but it is not actually the original 66-0300. 66-0370 went to the Turkish Air Force in November 1987 and was assigned as a ground trainer (as E-370) at Gaziemir Air Base. (USAF)

Opposite above: F-4E 69-7234 of the 35th Fighter Wing at George Air Force Base, California on 1 April 1982 during Exercise 'Gallant Eagle 82'. This Phantom was leased to the Royal Australian Air Force from 1970-73 as A69-7234. Damaged in a landing accident on 19 October 1970 at Amberley Queensland, it was repaired and re-flown in September 1971. Returning to USAF on 25 October 1972, it was modified as F-4G in September 1978, finally going to AMARC (as FP761) on 20 September 1991 and was converted to a QF-4G drone (AF212) on 31 August 1999. It was expended on 21 July 2005. (USAF)

Opposite below: F-4C 64-0727 releasing a B83 nuclear bomb at Edwards Air Force Base on 23 August 1983 during the last flight of the B83 project. Armed, the B83 had a maximum yield of 1.2 megatons. This Phantom went to AMARC (as FP096) on 23 April 1990 and was salvaged on 19 May 2000. (USAF)

WW
AF
69 234

ED
727

Above: F-4D 65-0696 in the 119th 'Happy Hooligans', North Dakota Air National Guard intercepting a Soviet Tupolev Tu-95 'Bear' over the Arctic Ocean, during a flight to Keflavik, Iceland in 1983. Eight Tu-95s were intercepted by 119th FG pilots during the deployment to Iceland. 65-0696 was used by AVTEL with civil registration N402AV before moving to Heritage Air Park, Palmdale, California. The registration was cancelled by the FAA in September 2002. (USAF)

Opposite above: F-4D 65-0700 with an AGM-88A hi-speed-anti-radiation missile (HARM) near Eglin AFB in 1983. This Phantom went to AMARC (as FP306) on 20 September 1989 and was still on the AMARC inventory in 2008. (USAF)

Opposite below: F-4Ds of the 184th 'Jayhawks' Tactical Fighter Group in 1984. F-4D 66-7735 retired to AMARC (as FP0100) on 21 April 1988. (USAF)

Above: RF-4C 66-0459 seen here taking off from RAF Coltishall, Norfolk, crashed into the remote upland region of the Smokey Mountains near Gatlinburg, Tennessee on 4 January 1984. Captain David Greggs and his back seater, Captain Scott Miller were killed. (Author)

Opposite above: F-4D of the 704th Tactical Fighter Squadron, 924th Tactical Fighter Wing Texas AFRC trails its drag chute while being parked in a revetment during exercise 'Team Spirit '85' at Kunsan Air Base, South Korea in 1985. (USAF)

Opposite below: F-4E 71-1087 from the 3rd Tactical Fighter Wing, Clark Air Base, Philippines, drops a GBU-15(V)1/B modular glide bomb during 'Exercise Team Spirit '85'. This Phantom went to AMARC (as FP684) on 4 June 1991 and then to QF-4E drone duties (as 'AF264') at Holloman AFB. (USAF)

TX
66 7404

FN
AF 71 087

Above: F-4Es 68-0526 and 68-0512 assigned to the 512th and 526th Tactical Fighter Squadrons, 86th Tactical Fighter Wing, fly one of their last aerial missions on 20 March 1985. Both squadrons from Ramstein Air Base, Germany replaced their Phantoms with the F-16 Fighting Falcon. 68-0512 was piloted by Lieutenant Colonel Bruce Gillett and navigated by Captain Mike Craig. Lieutenant Colonel Tom Speelman was piloting 68-0526 with 1st Lieutenant John Rogers navigating. While with the 196th TFS, California ANG on 13 June 1990, 68-0512 was number two in the flight support of an RF-4C transition sortie from March AFB California. While practising an attacking manoeuvre on the RF-4C, which was in a low altitude defence reaction turn at low altitude, the F-4E went out of control and crashed near Shoshone, California killing Major Robert M. McGann and his navigator Captain Thomas M. Steed. 68-0526 went to the 108th TFW, New Jersey ANG on 1 October 1985 and to the South Korean Air Force on 16 September 1991. (USAF)

Opposite above: F-4E in the 497th Tactical Fighter Squadron, 51st Tactical Fighter Wing over Korea on 1 March 1986 during Exercise 'Team Spirit', a joint military training exercise of US Forces Korea and the Military of South Korea held between 1976 and 1993. The exercise was also scheduled from 1994 to 1996 but was cancelled during this time period as part of diplomatic efforts to encourage the Government of North Korea to disable the North Korean nuclear weapons programme. (USAF)

Opposite below: F-4C 63-7644 of the 196th TFS, 193rd TFG California ANG at March AFB in 1987, the same year that this Phantom was put on display at Arnold AFB, Manchester, Tullahoma, Tennessee. (USAF)

ACFT 297
GU
AF
69 497 TFS

AF
69 644

Above: F-4D 66-0243 of the Fighter Interceptor Squadron, 191st Tactical Reconnaissance Group, Selfridge Air National Guard Base, Michigan in flight on 17 July 1987. This Phantom went to AMARC (as FP286) on 20 July 1989 and was still on the AMARC inventory in 2008. (USAF)

Opposite above: F-4G 'Wild Weasel' 69-0248 from the 480th Tactical Fighter Squadron with a General Dynamics F-16C Fighting Falcon of the 52nd Tactical Fighter Wing over the German countryside on 1 June 1989. The F-16C is carrying an AIM-9L/M Sidewinder missile on its outer wing pylons and both aircraft are armed with AGM-88 HARM missiles. The F-4G also carries AIM-7 Sparrow missiles. Converted to F-4G in 1979, 69-69-0248 later went to AMARC (as FP1016) on 31 January 1996. It then went to Holloman AFB, New Mexico as QF-4G AF140 on 23 May 1997 and was expended in the test of a Patriot SAM near Holloman on 6 June 2002. (USAF)

Opposite below: F-4G 'Wild Weasel' armed with AGM-88 HARM missiles from the 81st Tactical Fighter Squadron, 52nd Tactical Fighter Wing is serviced on the flight line prior to departing for Sheikh Isa Air Base, Bahrain, during Operation 'Desert Shield' in late 1990. The F-4 remained in use by the US in the reconnaissance and 'Wild Weasel' (Suppression of Enemy Air Defences) roles in the 1991 Gulf War, finally leaving service in 1996. (USAF)

SP
52 TFW
SP
AF
69248
480 TFS

Above: F-4Es (nearest aircraft is 69-7201) in the 35th TFW over the Saudi Desert in 1991. One of seventeen F-4Es leased to the Royal Australian Air Force from 1970 to 1973 (as A69-7201), 69-7201 returned to the USAF in June 1973 and was modified in July 1978 to F-4G; it flew fifty combat missions in 'Desert Storm'. It went to AMARC (as FP828) on 20 March 1992 and became a QF-4G drone (AF205) on 10 March 1999. It was expended on 29 June 2004. (USAF)

Opposite above: RF-4C 64-1047 *Iraqi Scud Seeker*, one of the six RF-4C Phantoms of the 106th TRS 117th Reconnaissance Wing, ANG from Birmingham, Alabama which were used during 'Desert Storm' in 1991 by active-duty 192nd TRS 152nd Recce Group ANG from Reno, Nevada. *Iraqi Scud Seeker* flew 172 sorties in 'Desert Shield'/'Desert Storm'. In daylight these unique RF-4Cs used their KS-127 LOROP (Long-Range Oblique Photography) cameras to spy on Iraqi forces from up to fifty miles away, looking for Scuds. This aircraft is preserved at USAF Museum, Wright Patterson AFB, Ohio. (Author)

Opposite below: F-4E 74-1650 in the 561st Fighter Squadron at George AFB in 1992 just before the unit's inactivation. This Phantom went to AMARC (as FP650) on 8 April 1991 and was still on the AMARC inventory in 2008. (USAF)

DY
IRAQI SCUD SEEKER
PULL HANDLE TO JETTISON CANOPIES
RESCUE
TOP SORTIE FLYER
DESERT SHIELD / STORM
172 SORTIES
Crew Chief: Len Naughen
Asst: Mark Bryant

WW
650

The 82nd Aerial Targets Squadron at Tyndall Air Force Base, Florida is the only remaining unit in the USAF still flying the F-4 Phantom and is reduced to the role of QF-4 aerial targets. The 82nd ATRS provides drone targets such as the QF-4 in the Full Scale Aerial Target role next to the MQM-107 Streaker and BQM-34 Firebee as Sub-Scale Aerial Targets. The 82 ATRS also has a Detachment at Holloman AFB which is responsible for FSAT operations at the White Sands Missile Range near Holloman AFB, New Mexico. The QF-4 has primary and back-up Automatic Flight Control System, Command/Telemetry System, VDOPS Scoring System, Flight Termination System, Visual Enhancement System and Ancillary Subsystems. The NULLO (Not Under Live Local Operation) full-scale Aerial Target flight always required at least three drones, the one to be shot down, a spare and a manned QF-4 flying as chase plane. The manned full-scale drones are fitted with advanced counter-measure systems and the rear cockpit ejection seat removed. All NULLO aircraft have both ejection seats removed. In November 2012 at a 123,000-square-foot hangar in Mojave, California, BAE Systems (the sole provider of QF-4s for the Air Force since 1996) successfully converted its 300th F-4 Phantom into an unmanned flying drone for the US Air Force.

CHAPTER 3

On Her Majesty's Service

The UK was the first export customer for the Phantom when in July 1964, the first British orders were placed with McDonnell Douglas for a deck-landing version of the F.4K (designated FG.Mk.1 in British service) for the Royal Navy to replace the Sea Vixen. In June 1965 it was also decided to order it for the RAF under the designation F-4M after the cancellation of the Hawker Siddeley P.1154 Mach 2 V/STOL fighter. The RAF was less than enthusiastic as the Phantom was primarily designed to operate in the air defence rather than the close air support role, and had been selected as its Hunter replacement more as a way of decreasing the per-unit cost of the overall UK order. An initial contract was placed for two YF-4Ms and two F-4K-27 production aircraft. The original Royal Navy order was for fifty F-4Ks, increased to 140 on the cancellation of the P.1154, but cuts in the carrier fleet resulted in a reduction to 120 and then eighty and then sixty and finally to only forty-eight (plus four development aircraft). All were re-engined with Rolls-Royce Spey turbofans in place of the J79 turbojets, and versions for the Royal Navy were fitted with a folding nose radome to fit RN hangar lifts, larger flaps, drooping ailerons and slotted tailplane with reduced anhedral. These modifications improved catapult performance and reduced approach speed by 10 mph, as well as improving radius of action, ferry range, take-off, climb and acceleration. However, the development cost for the changes to accommodate the Spey turbofans meant that the per-unit price eventually ended up three times the price of an F-4J.

The first F.4K (FG.1) for the Royal Navy made its maiden flight on 27 June 1966 and deliveries to the service began in April 1968. On 14 January 1969, the Phantom Training Unit, 767 Squadron, was formed to train crews for 892 Squadron, the first operational unit, which embarked in HMS *Ark Royal* on 12 June 1970 after operations from the USS *Saratoga* in the Mediterranean. One of 892's Phantoms from RNAS Yeovilton (XT858 '001')won the *Daily Mail* Transatlantic Air Race on 11 May 1969 (commemorating the 50th anniversary of Alcock and Brown's crossing of the Atlantic), setting a record for flight time from New York to London of 4 hours 46 minutes and 57 seconds. No.892 Squadron's Phantoms served in *Ark Royal* until the carrier was retired from service in 1978, when the Phantoms were turned over to the RAF and used to form a second squadron at Leuchars. At the time, 111

Squadron was stationed there operating the FGR.2 version of the Phantom, having been there since 1975. In 1979, to save costs resulting from the differences between the FG.1 and FGR.2, 'Treble One' converted onto the ex-FAA aircraft and the FGR.2 airframes were distributed to other Phantom units.

The first RAF Phantom made its maiden flight at St. Louis on 17 February 1967. The RAF operated the FG.1 in the air defence interceptor role and the FGR.2 in the UK on ground attack and tactical reconnaissance duties. Both 43 and 111 Squadrons retained the FG.1 until 1989 when they converted to the new Tornado F.3. Following the standing down of the two operational squadrons and the final withdrawal of the type from service, the bulk of the RAF's FG.1 Phantoms was scrapped. The first operational unit to be equipped with the FGR.2 was 6 Squadron at Coningsby in May 1969. The type equipped a further ten RAF squadrons. The FG.1 first entered service on 43 Squadron at Leuchars in September 1969. The twenty FG.1s supplied to the RAF were followed by 118 FGR.2s which were deployed to RAF Germany from July 1970. The RAF used the FGR.2 in the air defence role on 19 and 92 Squadrons in Germany and 23, 29, 56 and 111 Squadrons in the UK air defence force. These squadrons were complemented by FG.1.s on 43 Squadron which had special responsibility for the defence of naval forces. With the introduction of the Jaguar ground attack aircraft into squadron service, the strike Phantoms were gradually switched to the interceptor role where they replaced almost all Lightnings in service in Strike Command.

In May 1982 three Phantoms on 29 Squadron were forward deployed to RAF Wideawake on Ascension Island to provide air cover for the RAF's operations during the Falklands War, replacing Harriers of 1 Squadron, which were transiting to the war zone. In August 1982, following the end of the conflict and the reconstruction of the runway, 29 Squadron detached a number of its aircraft to RAF Stanley to provide air defence for the Falkland Islands. Late the following year, 23 Squadron took up the role, remaining stationed there until October 1988 when they were replaced by 1435 Flight. To make up for the loss of an entire squadron from the UK Air Defence Region, the RAF procured fifteen F-4Js that had previously been used by the US Navy. These aircraft were operated by 74 Squadron from 1984 until 1991 when they were replaced by FGR.2 Phantoms that had been released by other squadrons following their conversion to the Tornado. Initially it was intended that Phantoms and Tornadoes serve alongside each other. A total of 152 Tornado F.3s were ordered for the RAF; this was enough to convert four squadrons of Phantoms and two of Lightnings, but insufficient to completely convert every air defence squadron.

Both 23 and 29 Squadrons converted from the FGR.2 to the Tornado between 1987 and 1988 alongside the conversion of the final two remaining Lightning squadrons. The intention was to retain a pair of UK-based Phantom squadrons at RAF Wattisham, alongside a pair of Tornado units at RAF Coningsby to provide air defence cover for the southern half of the UK Air Defence Region. The end of the Cold War and the Options for Change defence review resulted in the two Germany-based units being disbanded but just prior to the final withdrawal of the Phantom, it was recalled operationally as a result of Operation 'Granby', the UK's participation in the First Gulf War. Six Phantoms on 19 and 92 Squadrons were forward deployed to provide air defence cover at RAF Akrotiri in place of Tornadoes that had been originally deployed there on exercise and were subsequently sent to the Gulf region. In 1992, with a few exceptions, the bulk of the RAF's FGR.2 fleet was scrapped. Throughout twenty years of service, the RAF lost eight of their FG.1s and thirty-seven FGR.2s in crashes.

The air and ground crews of the first F4M Phantom FGR.2 in RAF service (XT891) pose in front of their aircraft with Group Captain Stanley Mason at RAF Aldergrove, Northern Ireland on 20 July 1968. XT891 first flew on 26 December 1967. It ended its service career as an airfield decoy (9136M) at RAF Coningsby, Lincolnshire.

Above: EKA-3B Skywarrior (BuNo142255) of Det.60, VAH-10 'Vikings' assigned to the aircraft carrier USS *Saratoga*, refuelling an 892 Naval Air Squadron Phantom FG.1 ('013') from HMS *Ark Royal* in 1969. (USAF)

Opposite above: Phantoms on 228 Squadron at RAF Coningsby, Lincolnshire in 1969. The first FGR.2 arrived on the OCU on 9 September 1968.

Opposite below: FG.1 (F-4K) XV590 '007' during Exercise 'Northern Wedding' in the Arctic in 1970. In December 1978, this Phantom was transferred to the RAF, being retired and then scrapped in 1992.

905
420

R
ROYAL NAVY
07

Above: FGR.2 XT907 at NAS Patuxent River in about 1970. This Phantom was delivered to the RAF on 25 July 1969. It became an airfield decoy (9151M) at RAF Bentwaters on 3 July 2014.

Opposite above: FG.1 Phantoms on 43 Squadron passing the Forth Bridge. The 'Fighting Cocks' reformed at Leuchars on 1 September 1969 with the Phantom, which it flew until its replacement by the Tornado F.3 in September 1989. Whereas most RAF Phantom squadrons were flying the FGR.2, the two Leuchars squadrons (Nos. 43 and 111) operated the FG.1. RAF Leuchars was the shore base for the *Ark Royal's* F-4 Phantoms. Among the numerous differences between the two marks, the FGR.2, unlike the FG.1, had a HF radio, INAS (Inertial Navigation and Attack System) and an internal battery. The FG.1 had slotted stabilators (slab tailplanes) for added manoeuvrability and all the carrier launch equipment. It was known to its pilots as the 'North Sea Sports GT model'.

Opposite below: FGR.2 XV424 on 29 Squadron, which was delivered to the RAF on 12 February 1969 and is now displayed at the RAF Museum, Hendon. From May 1967, 29 Squadron operated the English Electric Lightning F.3 at RAF Wattisham in Suffolk until December 1974 when they re-equipped with the F-4 Phantom and moved to RAF Coningsby in Lincolnshire. A detachment was stationed at Wideawake airstrip on Ascension Island during the Falklands War, moving on to provide defence of the Falklands in August 1982, following repairs to the airfield at Stanley. In 1987, 29 Squadron was one of the first RAF units to receive the Tornado F.3.

XV424

FGR.2s on 14 Squadron in RAF Germany passing Schlöss Hohenzollern in 1972. In June 1970, 14 Squadron had moved to RAF Brüggen to become the first unit in RAF Germany to be equipped with the FGR2. With supersonic performance and a pulsed-doppler air-to-air radar, the Phantom provided a considerable improvement to the Squadron's operational capability. The Phantom era set the pattern for the next twenty years: maintenance of the nuclear strike role and training for both nuclear and conventional operations within the low flying system in Germany. Additionally, annual Armament Practice camps were held at the Quadri-national Training Base at Decimomannou in Sardinia. Shortly after becoming operational with the Phantom, 14 Squadron won the Salmond Trophy, a highly prestigious bombing and navigation competition between the flying Squadrons in RAF Germany. The Phantom was replaced by the Sepecat Jaguar GR1 aircraft in 1975, making 14 Squadron the first-ever single-seat strike squadron in the RAF.

FG.1 '014' on 892 Squadron on HMS *Ark Royal* on 2 March 1972. The UK was the only country outside the United States to operate the Phantom at sea.

Above: FG.1 XT871 '007' being catapulted from HMS *Ark Royal*. During the Phantom's service with the Royal Navy, ten of the total FAA fleet of twenty-eight were lost in crashes. On 25 July 1973, XT871 on return to Rosyth launched from *Ark Royal*, but engine failure caused the aircraft to crash off the bow into the Firth of Forth and the crew had to be rescued by a SAR Wessex helicopter. XV589, one of twenty FG.1s transferred to the RAF, suffered a mishap on 3 June 1980 while on 111 Squadron detached from RAF Leuchars for training purposes during a routine flight to RAF Alconbury. As the aircraft neared the airfield and lined up for the runway at approximately 350 feet altitude, the nose section radome was seen to open. This sudden resultant drag factor caused the aircraft to roll and yaw. Despite attempts to correct these problems, Flight Lieutenants P. R. Watling and S. L. James had no option but to eject. They both landed safely and suffered slight injuries. Over its service life, thirty-seven FGR.2s were lost to crashes.

Opposite above: FG.1 (F-4K) '010' of 892 Naval Air Squadron builds up power to launch from the USS *Independence* during the NATO exercise 'Ocean Safari' in November 1975. The fierce heat from the Spey's afterburners required the installation of special water-cooled jet blast deflectors aboard *Ark Royal* to avoid extensive damage to the flight deck.

Opposite below: 892 Squadron FG.1 '114' with the unit's 'Omega' insignia on its fin, launches from HMS *Ark Royal* with a load of ten 1,000 lb bombs. (RN)

R
ROYAL NAVY

014
14

Above: FG.1 XV574/B on 43 Squadron 'The Fighting Cocks' from RAF Leuchars intercepting a Tu-20 'Bear-D' engaged in a probe mission in 1975. The Phantom was better suited to long-range interceptions over the North Sea than the ubiquitous Lightning. XV574 was delivered to the RAF on 14 February 1969. It was scrapped at Wattisham in September 1991.

Opposite above: 892 Squadron at RAF Leuchars in1976 getting ready to deploy to *Ark Royal*.

Opposite below: FGR.2 (F-4M) XV408 on 23 Squadron at RAF Finningley on 30 July 1977. On 12 December 1968, XV408 was one of the first Phantoms delivered to the RAF, serving briefly on 228 OCU at Coningsby and in June 1969 being allocated to 6 Squadron, the first operational Phantom unit, for fighter/ground attack duties. XV408 saw further service with the OCU between 1974 and 1976 at which point, with this aircraft type switching to the air defence role, it was transferred to 23 Squadron. Moves between several squadrons in both the UK and Germany followed until 1992 when XV408 was finally retired. After a year in storage, XV408 became a gate guardian at Cranwell and was later displayed in the open at Halton and Fairford. Faced with being scrapped in 2004, the RAF Museum agreed to take on the aircraft as a gift and offer it on permanent loan to the Tangmere Military Aviation Museum.

ROYAL NAVY
001
002
003
R

Above: FGR.2 XV435 on 92 Squadron at RAF Wildenrath in 1979. This Phantom was delivered on 24 May 1969 and ended its service life at RAE Llanbedr, Wales and it was consigned to the fire dump in 1992, being scrapped in December 2004.

Opposite above: FGR.2 XV464 on 56 Squadron from RAF Wattisham, having landed at RAF Akrotiri following gunnery practice in Cyprus in November 1980. This Phantom was delivered to the RAF on 25 April 1969. It was scrapped at Wattisham in February 1992.

Opposite below: 123.1 FGR.2 on 43 Squadron approaching a USAF KC-135A tanker of the 306th Strategic Wing for in-flight refuelling on 1 September 1980.

B

After the Falklands War, 23 Squadron was deployed to Port Stanley to guard against further Argentine aggression, which left a gap in the UK's air defence. As a stop-gap measure, 74 Squadron was reformed on 30 August 1984 and during 1984-85, fifteen low hours ex-US Navy/Marine F-4Js, which had been extensively refurbished and stored at Davis-Monthan AFB's AMARG 'boneyard', were flown to RAF Wattisham. The F-4J was chosen due to its compatibility with the F-4K and F-4M (FG.1 and FGR.2). F-4J BuNo153783/ZE352 crewed by Commander Steve Queen RIO and Flight Lieutenant Clive Bairstow, seen here in 1984 near San Diego, California, was delivered to Wattisham on 30 August 1984. Once of VX-4 Air Test and Evaluation Squadron at NAS Point Magu in California, BuNo153783 was known as 'Black Bunny' due to its paint scheme and the 'Playboy' rabbit that appeared on its tail fin during the 1960s until the F-14 took over in the early 1970s. The only F-4J loss occurred on 26 August 1987 when ZE358 (155510) flew into a slight ridge at Pant-y-Gwair, ten miles SE of Aberystwyth, Dyfed during low level intercept practice with two other Phantoms. Both the pilot, Flight Lieutenant Euan Holm Murdoch and navigator, Flying Officer Jeremy Lindsey Ogg were killed. The fourteen remaining ex-US Navy F-4Js were finally withdrawn from RAF service in January 1991. BuNo155529 (ZE359), resplendent in VF-74 markings it wore on the USS *America* for war cruise 5 June 1972-24 March 1973 during 'Linebacker' (it flew eighty-eight combat hours during the Viêtnam War), is at the Imperial War Museum at Duxford. ZE360 (BuNo155574), Britain's only other complete F-4J, is at the Defence Fire Training School at Manston in Kent.

When in January 1991 74 Squadron gave up their F-4J Phantoms, they received surplus FGR.2s before disbanding in October 1992 when RAF Wattisham began its transition to the Army Air Corps. XV474/T nearest the camera was last flown on 13 October 1992 to IWM Duxford.

F-4K (FG.1) XV574 on 111 Squadron at RAF Greenham Common in July 1983. In 1974 'Treble One' moved from RAF Wattisham after almost eighteen years and re-equipped with the F-4 at RAF Coningsby, before moving north to Leuchars on 3 November 1975. The RAF took delivery of XV574 on 14 February 1969, the aircraft finally being scrapped at Wattisham in September 1991.

Above: FGR.2 on 1435 Flight being air-to-air refuelled in 1991. In November 1988, when 23 Squadron converted to the Tornado, 1435 Flight was revived at RAF Mount Pleasant, equipped with four FGR.2s, providing air defence for the Falkland Islands, South Georgia and the South Sandwich Islands. After 23 Squadron's disbandment at Mount Pleasant, the mission and equipment were transferred to 1435 Flight, flying the Panavia Tornado F.3 and later the Eurofighter Typhoon.

Opposite above: 56 and 74 Squadron Phantom flypast over London in 1992 (note the 'Snoopy' in the FCP of the bottom left Phantom). XV433 last flew on 6 October 1992 to RAF Shawbury for storage and it was scrapped in August 1995. Following a four year stay in Cyprus, 56 Squadron converted to Phantoms in 1976, finally retiring the last of these in July 1992 when 65 (R) Squadron, the Tornado F3 Operational Conversion Unit at Coningsby, was re-named 56 (R) Squadron.

Opposite below: FGR.2 XV501 on 92 Squadron at Wildenrath in 1977 with Squadron Commander Wing Commander 'Black' Ferguson and navigator Paul Pike setting out on another sortie. Note the 111 Squadron and 43 Squadron zaps. This Phantom was delivered on 29 October 1969 and withdrawn from use on 2 August 1988.

Above: FGR.2 XV482 on 54 Squadron, which was delivered on 4 August 1969 to Leuchars, Scotland and was finally scrapped in 1995. The FGR.2's 'warload' consisted of drop tanks, four or six rocket launchers, two or three Sparrow missiles and a SUU-23/A ventral gun pod or a centreline reconnaissance pod and two ECM units.

Opposite above: FGR.2 XV465 on 92 Squadron of RAF Germany on exercise in Belgium in the early 1980s. This Phantom was delivered on 3 October 1969 and finally scrapped in August 1991.

Opposite below: FGR.2 XV481 on 56 Squadron on full afterburner for take-off. This Phantom was also used on 19 Squadron at RAF Wildenrath during 1984-85 and on 23 Squadron at Mount Pleasant in the Falkland Islands in 1987, and is now on static display at Hurn.

465
EDB
3703 4

CHAPTER 4

International Operators

Iran received approximately 225 F-4Ds, E's and RF-4Es from the United States prior to the Iranian Revolution of 1979. In 1966 the Nirou Havai Shahanshahiye Iran (Imperial Iranian Air Force or IIAF) ordered sixteen F-4Ds; the first of which arrived on 8 September 1968, with another sixteen added later and were employed in several unsuccessful attempts to intercept Soviet MiG-25Rs. The F-4Ds were also used for ground attack and during one such mission, rebels in Oman shot one down. In 1970 the first RF-4Es were delivered, followed by an order for 177 F-4Es, the first of which arrived in March 1971. During a border clash in June 1975, these F-4s, armed with AGM-65 Maverick missiles, defeated an Iraqi armoured ground formation. The F-4Es changed the balance of power in the region for they were not only effective on the battlefield, but were also available in large numbers. During 1974-77, a total of 177 F-4Es and sixteen RF-4Es were delivered. Following the overthrow of the Shah in 1979, thirty-one of the F-4Es and sixteen of the undelivered RF-4Es were embargoed by the US and placed in storage at Davis-Monthan AFB. After the Iranian Revolution of 1979, the US placed an armament embargo, preventing Iran from acquiring further spare parts to keep the fleet flying, and purges greatly weakened the air force leaving the 180 Phantoms still in service largely without trained air and ground crews. When in September 1980 Iraqi forces invaded Iran, the renamed Islamic Republic of Iran Air Force (IRIAF) was ill-prepared to meet the threat. But during the nine-year-long war, the Phantom reportedly acquitted itself well against Iraqi MiG-23s and carried out several long-range raids on the Iraqi airfields, though the actual number of air-to-air kills remains disputed. Iran is believed to have benefited from foreign assistance with clandestine shipments of up to twenty-three new airframes plus spares from the US and Israel, as well as from locally designed and reverse-engineered components and weapons and incorporation of ex-Soviet and Chinese technology. The Phantom of an Iranian pilot who deserted on 31 August 1984 to Saudi Arabia was examined and found to have Israeli and European spare parts fitted. By 1985, only about fifty of the original 225 Phantoms were still serviceable and in 1988, only a small handful of F-4Es and RF-4Es remained. Iranian F-4s were in use as of late 2014, the aircraft reportedly conducting air strikes on ISIS targets in the eastern Iraqi province of Diyala.

In South Korea in 1969, the Han-guk Kong Goon (RoKAF) obtained eighteen ex-USAF F-4Ds under the 'Peace Spectator' programme to replace the F-86D. In 1972 the RoKAF transferred its F-5A/Bs to the Viêtnamese Air Force and in return received eighteen additional F-4Ds to re-equip another squadron. Six F-4Ds were supplied later by the USAF as attrition replacements and during 1987-88, twenty-four further ex-USAF F-4Ds were acquired to bring the RoKAF's two F-4D squadrons back to strength and to equip a third. During 1977-79, thirty-seven new F-4Es were delivered under 'Peace Pheasant II'. In 1988-89, seventy-six ex-USAF F-4Es (and twelve ex-USAF RF-4Cs) arrived and the RoKAF had formed its fifth F-4E squadron by the end of 1989. In total, South Korea has received 216 Phantoms.

On 1 July 1968, Israel and the US signed the 'Peace Echo' agreement for the supply of fifty F-4Es and six RF-4Es. These entered service with three squadrons in 1969. The F-4 saw extensive use in Israeli service, scoring 116 air-to-air kills against the Egyptian and Syrian air forces, starting in 1969 during the War of Attrition. In total, the IDF/AF received 240 F-4Es, including eighty-six ordered under FMS contracts and aircraft transferred from the USAF inventory. Following increased tension in the region, on 22 October 1969, just six weeks after the Phantoms entered service, the F-4Es went into action with strikes against SAM missile sites in Egypt. Finally, an American-sponsored ceasefire came into effect on 7 August 1970. By 1973 the IDF/AF had 432 aircraft in its inventory, of which Phantoms were the second most numerous aircraft, against 600 aircraft operated by Egypt and 210 by Syria. In the Yom Kippur War, Israel admitted to total losses of 115 aircraft (US estimates were nearer 200), sixty of them in the first week of the War. An armistice was agreed on 24 October 1973 and Operation 'Nickle Grass' ensured that Israeli losses were made good with the urgent delivery of thirty-six F-4Es from USAFE and TAC units. By the end of the 1970s, 110 F-4Es still equipped five squadrons but most of the Phantoms were high-time aircraft and it was not cost-effective to modernise them. In 1982 in Operation 'Mole Cricket 19' during Israel's intervention in the War in Lebanon, Phantoms escorted by new F-15s and F-16s destroyed all thirty of Syria's SAM batteries in the Beka'a Valley in one day without losing a single aircraft. In the 1980s, Israel began the 'Kurnass 2000' modernisation programme which significantly updated avionics. The last Israeli F-4s were retired in 2004.

Towards the end of the 1960s, the Federal German Republic began seeking a replacement aircraft for its Lockheed F-104G/RF-104G Starfighter force. In January 1969, eighty-eight RF-4Es were ordered for the Luftwaffe, the first RF-4E flying on 15 September 1970. On 16 January 1971, this aircraft (named Spirit of St Louis) and three others, departed St. Louis for West Germany. Further deliveries (of forty-two RF-4Es each) were made to two tactical reconnaissance Geschwader, Aufk.

larungsgeschwader 51 (AG 51) Immelmann' at Bremgarten and AG 52 at Leek, where they replaced RF-104G Starfighters. Two aircraft were delivered to Erprobungsstelle 61 for trials and two others to TSLW 1 at Kaufbeuren for training. By the 1970s, changes in the MRCA-75 (Panavia Tornado) programme that deleted the single-seat version originally specified by the Luftwaffe and put back delivery of the two-seat version, opened up a gap in West Germany's fighter inventory. As a result, in 1971 the Bundestag Defence Committee ordered 175 F-4Fs as part of the 'Peace Rhine' programme to replace the F-104G in two Jagdgeschwader (fighter wings; thirty F-4Fs each) and two Jagdbombergeschwader (fighter- bomber wings; thirty-six F-4Fs each). The first F-4F flew in May 1975 and deliveries to JG 71 'Richthofen' at Wittmundhafen and JG 74 'Mölders at Neuburg began in June that year. (In German service, the Phantom became known as the 'Elefunt' because of its large intakes!) Conversion training for Luftwaffe RF-4E and F-4F crews meanwhile was carried out at George AFB in California within the 35th TFW under a US/West German co-operative agreement. Fifteen of the 175 F-4Fs produced between May 1973 and April 1976 were retained for the training phase until replaced in 1977 by ten F-4Es paid for by West Germany, but delivered to the USAF for use by the 20th TFS at George AFB. In 1974, JBG 36 began conversion to the F-4F at Rheine-Hopsten and by mid-1976, 361 and 362 Staffeln were operational. During 1981 a third component, the Zentrale Ausbilddung-seinrichtung (ZAE, 363 Staffel) was added to the wing. The ZAE was assigned to 'Europeanisation' conversion of pilots who learned to fly the F-4F at George AFB and who were unused to the European weather and airspace restrictions. On 11 April 1975, JBG 35 at Pferdsfeld flew its last Fiat G.91 sorties and began conversion to the F-4F.

In 1982 the RF-4Es were given a secondary ground-attack role and were updated with improved sensors (such as IR linescan) and an optical sight. JG 71's and JG 74's F-4Fs were modernised in the early 1990s under the ICE (Improved Combat Efficiency) programme. Both JBG 35's and JBG 36's F-4Fs also received upgrades. The original plan was to upgrade seventy-five F-4Fs, but the number was increased to 110 in the late 1980s. Initially, the ICE upgrades were intended only for the interceptor wings, but more were upgraded due to delays in the Eurofighter Typhoon programme. By 1990 Phantom losses were twenty-one F-4Fs and fifteen RF-4Es.

The ICE F-4Fs were expected to remain in service until JG 71 transitioned to the Eurofighter Typhoon in 2013. JG 73 retired its last F-4F in 2002 and replaced it with Eurofighters in 2003, while the last F-4F left JG-74 in March 2008. The remaining F-4F wings were disbanded without replacement during the 1990s and early 2000s. The Luftwaffe retired its last operational F-4F on 29 June 2013.

In Australia the delivery of twenty-four F-111C aircraft to replace its Australian-built Canberra B.Mk.20 bombers was scheduled for 1968, but the onset of fatigue problems with the F-111 meant that the US would seriously delay service entry, leaving the RAAF without attack aircraft; on 22 June 1970 the US diverted twenty-four F-4Es from USAF production contracts to equip Nos. 1 and 6 Squadrons of 82 (Bomber) Wing at Amberley, Brisbane. Late in 1972, eleven of the F-4Es were returned to the USAF with the last twelve leaving Australia in June 1973.

In 1971 the Ejército del Aire Espanol (Spanish Air Force or EdA) sought to replace its F-104Gs with the F-4C. From October 1971 to September 1972, the EdA received thirty-six F-4Cs from USAFE's 81st TFW. Each aircraft (some of which had already been used in the war in South-East Asia) was completely overhauled at the Construcciones Aeronauticas SA (CASA) plant at Getafe and delivered to the EdA with the Spanish designation C.12. All were used to equip the newly commissioned Escuadrón 121 at Torrejón and later Esc 122 (after Esc 104 disbanded). Four F-4Cs were lost in accidents and were replaced, in July and August 1978, by ex-USAF F-4Cs from the 35th TFW and 58th Tactical Training Wing (TTW). Four RF-4Cs arrived from October to November 1978 and were designated CR.12 in EdA service. During the winter of 1988, the C.12s of Esc 121 and Esc 122 at Torrejón were replaced by the C.15 (EF-18 Hornet). In January 1989, eight ex-Kentucky ANG RF-4Cs arrived to join the four original CR.12s to enable the EdA to form a specialised tactical reconnaissance squadron. Spain retired its CR.12s in 2002.

In Japan in July 1971, two F-4EJ pattern prototype aircraft were delivered to the Nihon Kōkū Jieitai (Japan Air Self-Defence Force or JASDF) and during the Fourth Defence Build-up Programme (DBP), orders were placed with Mitsubishi Heavy Industries at Nagoya for 128 production aircraft. Eleven F-4EJs were also assembled in Japan. After evaluation by the Kōkū Jikkendan (Air Proving Wing) at Komaki, F-4EJs were assigned on 1 August 1972 to the Rinji (Provisional) 301 Hikōtai (Squadron) as part of 6 Kōkūdan (Air Wing) at Nyutabaru. The F-4EJ entered service with a total of six Hikōtai (Squadrons) operating the aircraft. In October 1973, 301 Hikōtai became a fully fledged squadron in 5 Kōkūdan. F-4EJs were assigned to four other Hikotais; 302 in 7 Kokudan at Naha, 303 of 6 Kokudan at Komatsu, 304 at Tsuiki in 7 Kōkūdan and, in 1977, 305 at Hyakuri on Okinawa as part of the S-W Mixed Air Wing. Upgraded F-4EJ KAIs entered service with 306 Hikotai in November 1989. The RF-4EJ equipped the 501st Hikōtai of the Teisatsu Kōkūtai (Tactical Reconnaissance Group) at Hyakuri that had previously operated the RF-86F. Due to Japanese military limitations prohibiting air-to-ground ordnance, the F-4EJs were delivered without the AN/AJB-7 bombing computer system and also did not have an air-refuelling probe or receptacle. In service, F-4EJs replaced the JASDF's fleet of Lockheed F-104J Starfighters. McDonnell-Douglas built the two prototype F-4EJs, which first flew on 14 January 1971. The next eleven aircraft were assembled in Japan and the first Japanese-built example flew on 12 May 1972. Mitsubishi built all the EJs over the next nine years and the production ended with 127th F-4EJ on 20 May 1981. This was the last F-4 built in the world.

As of 2007, Japan had a fleet of ninety F-4s in service. In June that year, Lockheed Martin announced that the company had been awarded a contract to equip several F-15 Eagles with synthetic aperture radar pods that would be used in a reconnaissance role, allowing the RF-4EJ to be retired. After studying several replacement fighters including the Eurofighter Typhoon, the F-35 Lightning II was chosen in 2011 to replace the F-4EJ. Delays with the F-35 programme, however, meant that some F-4s remained in service. As of 2017, all three of the JASDF's remaining Phantom squadrons were based at Hyakuri Air Base in Ibaraki Prefecture, north of Tokyo. Some F-4EJs were also operated by the Air Development and Test Wing in Gifu Prefecture.

The Hellenic Air Force (PA - Polemikí Aeroporía) took delivery of thirty-eight F-4Es under 'Peace Icarus' in March 1974 to equip 117 Ptérix Mahis (Combat Wing), 28th Taktiki Aeroporiki Dynamis (Tactical Air Force) at Andravida. The first eighteen Greek Phantoms entered in service in 338° 'Aias' Mira (Squadron) in the ground-attack role and 339° 'Aias' Mira in the air-to-air role, and also as the operational training unit. Turkey's invasion of Cyprus in July found 339° 'Aias' Mira still in training, but it was decided to send ten Phantoms fully loaded with weapons to Crete to assume action against the landing forces. However, the fragile political situation saw 339° 'Aias' Mira's missions cancelled and the Greek forces fighting in Cyprus were deprived of the deterrent potential of the F-4 - a type that the Turkish Air Force did not yet possess. In 1976, two more F-4Es were delivered to the HAF to replace losses and in May 1978, deliveries of the second F-4E procurement contract ('Peace Icarus II') began; all eighteen aircraft were delivered during 1978-79. This second batch of Phantoms enabled the establishment of a third F-4 unit, 337° Mira 'Ghost' based at Larissa. This unit would assume primary responsibility for the defence of the central and northern Aegean. Also in 1978 the first of eight RF-4Es were delivered to 348° 'Eyes' Mira Taktikis Anagnoriseos of 110 Ptérix Mahis at Larissa, completing the original Phantom orders for the HAF. In 1991 the HAF accepted twenty-eight F-4Es from the Indiana Air National Guard under the South-eastern Regional Agreement (SRA). With their introduction, all F-4s from the original Greek orders were allocated between 337° Mira 'Ghost' and 339° 'Aias' Mira, while 338° 'Ares' Mira received all the ex-ANG Phantoms. Though the SRA F-4s were from older production blocks, they featured the advanced Navigation and Weapon-Delivery System (NWDS), Airborne Video Tape Recorder (AVTR), Have Quick radios and improvements to the AN/APQ-120 radar to make it more capable in the air-to-ground role. Two years later, the 348° Mira fleet was enhanced by twenty-nine RF-4Es from the German Luftwaffe.

On 11 August 1997, a contract was signed with EADS for the 'Peace Icarus 2000' upgrade, also known as the Avionics Upgrade Programme (AUP) to a similar standard as the Luftwaffe F-4F ICE, including APG-65 radar, a GEC-Marconi HUD and GPS/INS. It was decided to upgrade the Phantoms obtained under 'Peace Icarus I' and 'Peace Icarus II' and to apply a Service-Life Extension Programme (SLEP) to the entire F-4 and RF-4 fleet. A first AUP-upgraded F-4 was delivered in December 2002. In total, thirty-eight aircraft were upgraded, thirty-seven of them by Hellenic Aerospace Industry, at Tanagra. In 2005, 337° Mira retired the F-4E SRA jets and replaced these with F-16s, the squadron again assuming its role as lead interception unit in the northern Aegean. As of September 2013, Greece was operating thirty-four upgraded F-4Es and a dozen RF-4E aircraft. On 5 May 2017, the Hellenic Air Force officially retired the RF-4E Phantom during a public ceremony. On 31 October 2017, an official ceremony was held at Andravida Air Base for the disbandment of 339° 'Aias' Mira and the personnel and their F-4E (AUP) aircraft merged with 338° 'Ares' Mira.

Beginning in August 1974, seventy-two F-4Es were delivered to the Turk Hava Kuvvetleri (THK, or Turkish Air Force) under 'Peace Diamond' III and IV. In 1977 the US Government approved the export of thirty-two more F-4Es and eight RF-4Es and by 1988, the THK had obtained forty-five ex-USAF F-4Es. Additional F-4Es from surplus US stocks followed during the late 1980s and early 1990s. Turkish F-4s remained in use as of 2015 and it is reported that F-4E 2020s were used against the Third Phase of the PKK conflict on heavy bombardment missions into Iraq on 15 November 2015, 12 January 2016 and 12 March 2016.

In 1980 the Al Quwwat al Jawwiya il Misriya (Arab Republic of Egypt Air Force) received thirty-five early production, ex-USAF F-4Es under the 'Peace Pharaoh' programme to re-equip two squadrons in the 222nd Tactical Fighter Brigade at Cairo-West. Unfortunately, the Phantoms, which had already seen considerable service, proved too difficult to maintain and in May 1982, they were flown back to the USA for major overhaul and reassignment to another air force. However, Egypt had a change of heart since plans were by now well advanced to equip the Arab Republic of Egypt Air Force with 120 F-16 Fighting Falcons and 120 F-5G Tigersharks. The F-4Es therefore remained in service with the two squadrons of the 222nd Fighter Regiment at Cairo-West until replacement by the newer types.

Operation 'Desert Storm' was the Phantom's swansong in battle. Though their numbers were few in a conflict viewed appropriately as the first real 'electronics war', fast-ageing F-4G Wild Weasels, crammed with avionics, performed superbly in a hunter-killer partnership with F-16s. Following the Gulf War, the 52nd TFW was assigned to Operation 'Southern Watch' to patrol the no-fly zone over southern Iraq on F-4G defence suppression/ destruction missions in conjunction with 'Wild Weasel' F-16C/Ds. In 1995, the only active-duty USAF unit flying F-4G Wild Weasel sorties was the 561st FS at Nellis AFB, Nevada. Major Tom Pfeiffer, one of the pilots, had flown over 130 F-4G missions over Iraq enforcing the no-fly zone, having scored a SAM site kill during 'Desert Storm'. Of firing a missile at a SAM radar, he recalled: 'There was a loud rumble that sounded like a bottle rocket going off, then whoosh! It comes off the wing. It's really exciting and after all the training and practice, I felt a real sense of accomplishment.' His father-in-law flew F-15s and before that was a 'Wild Weasel' pilot himself. Describing the no-fly zone missions, Pfeiffer said, 'Occasionally [the Iraqi troops] turn on their early warning radar to get a quick view of where we're flying. They've gotten quieter and quieter with each temporary-duty rotation. Sometimes we'll fly 24-hour operations and sometimes we'll have crews up for just a couple of hours or half a day. We try to keep them off balance so they can't predict when or where we'll be. We don't jam the enemy's radar, the only thing we jam are HARM missiles down the enemy's throat! Flying the F-4G is like driving a classic '68 Corvette. It's just fantastic! Sheer, raw power.'

What a superb epitaph for one of the world's truly great aircraft.

As of 2008, 631 Phantoms were in service worldwide, with redundant models operated in the US military being used as a target drone (specifically QF-4Cs) until 21 December 2016, when the Air Force officially ended use of the type. As of 2017, almost sixty years after its introduction, the F-4 remained in service with Iran, Japan, South Korea and Turkey, the aircraft most recently being seen in operations against the Islamic State group in the Middle East.

Opposite above: RAAF F-4E Phantoms 97213, 97214 and 97209 (69-7213, 69-7214 and 69-7209, respectively) in formation over Australia in March 1971. Twenty-four F-4Es were loaned to Australia to equip Nos. 1 and 6 Squadrons RAAF at Amberley, Brisbane. The survivors were returned to the USA late in June 1973 and all were among the aircraft converted to F-4G 'Wild Weasel' configuration for the USAF. (RAAF)

Opposite below: Nihon Kōkū Jieitai (Japan Air Self-Defence Force or JASDF) Mitsubishi F-4EJ Kai '435' and '425' 97-8425 of 302 Hikōtai (Squadron). The JASDF received a total of 154 F-4EJ aircraft, (twenty-seven of which were built by McDonnell-Douglas and 127 of which were built by Mitsubishi Heavy Industries under licence) and fourteen RF-4Es bought directly from McDonnell-Douglas. (JASDF)

97213
13
14

425
435
97-8425

Above: C.12 (RF-4C AN1337858) of the Ejército del Aire Espanol (Spanish Air Force or EdA), which received thirty-six ex-USAF F-4Cs between October 1971 and September 1972, with four more arriving between July and August 1978. The C.12s equipped Escuadrón 121 and Escuadrón 122 of Ala de Caza nº12 (12 Wing) at Torrejón, until the winter of 1988. (EdA)

Opposite above: F-4E 73-1023 of the Turk Hava Kuvvetleri (THK, or Turkish Air Force) over an air base in northern Jordan during a mission at Exercise 'Eager Lion' on 29 May 2014. Soldiers, sailors, airmen and marines from more than twenty partner nations came together for two weeks to enhance their interoperability while participating in air-, land- and sea-based scenarios. (USAF)

Opposite below: F-4E AUPs 72-1507 and 72-1504 of the Hellenic Air Force (PA - Polemikí Aeroporía). 72-1507 joined the Hellenic Air Force in May 1974 and was upgraded to F-4E AUP configuration; it was still in service in 2011. 72-1504 went to the Hellenic Air Force in March 1974, being written off on 27 May 1999. (HAF)

Above: A 347th Tactical Fighter Wing F-4E flying with F-4E 66-0366 of the 222nd Tactical Fighter Brigade Al Quwwat al Jawwiya il Misriya (Arab Republic of Egypt Air Force) during Exercise 'Proud Phantom'. 66-0366 joined the Egyptian Air Force in September 1979 as '7801'. (US National Archives)

Opposite above: F-4E of the Nirou Havai Shahanshahiye Iran (IIAF) taking off in 2009.

Opposite below: F-4E 68-0499 of the Han-guk Kong Goon (RoKAF) or South Korean Air Force in 1979. This Phantom went to AMARC (as FP640) on 2 April 1991 and was converted to a QF-4E drone at Tyndall AFB (as AF106) on 31 October 1995. It was expended as a target on 17 November 1999. (RoKAF)

IRIAF

499

Above: Deliveries to the Luftwaffe of F-4Fs (JG 74 pictured over Germany in 1998) to JG 71 'Richthofen' at Wittmundhafen and JG 74 'Mölders at Neuburg began in June 1975. (GAF)

Opposite above: MiG kill by Heyl ha'Avir (Israeli Air Force) F-4E Phantom pilot Major Moshe Meinick in the Yom Kippur War (6-25 October 1973). The Heyl ha'Avir lost thirty-three of its 140 F-4Es, mainly to SAMs. Israel admitted to total losses of 115 aircraft (US estimates were nearer 200), sixty of them in the first week of the war. (IAF)

Opposite below: The F-4E 'was introduced into the Heyl ha'Avir inventory in September of 1969. 201 squadrons, 'The One' ('HaAchat') and 69 'The Hammers' ('HaPatishim') initially flew the aircraft. In 1971, 119 Squadron became the third 'Kurnass' ('Sledgehammer') squadron to become operational. By 1978, 204 F-4Es had been delivered to the Heyl ha'Avir, of which about sixty-five had been lost in combat and operational accidents. In total the Heyl ha'Avir received 240 F-4Es including eighty-six Phantoms ordered under FMS contracts and F-4Es transferred from the USAF inventory. In total, only five squadrons ever flew the F-4 (201, 69, 119, 107 and 105). The IDF/AF Flight Test squadron borrowed F-4s from the operational squadrons to advance the capabilities of the 'Kurnass' by adding Israeli-designed modifications which included a fixed refuelling capability, weapon attachments and unique electronic warfare instruments. (IAF)

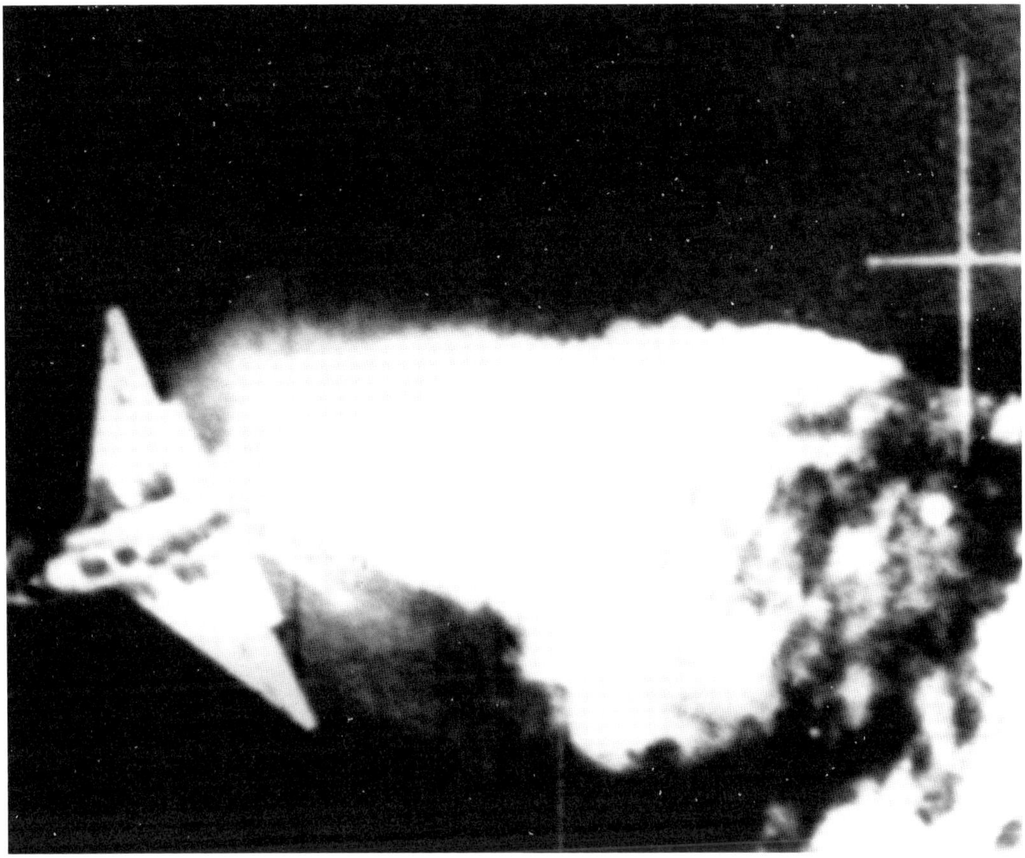